The BHS
Training Manual

RIGG COLLEGE
PENRITH

for re...

Stage 2

The BHS
Training Manual
FOR
Stage 2

The British Horse Society

Islay Auty FBHS

KENILWORTH PRESS

First published in 2004 by
Kenilworth Press Ltd
Addington
Buckingham
MK18 2JR

British Library Cataloguing in Publication Data
A catalogue record for this book is available from the British Library.

ISBN 0-872119-59-X

Layout by Kenilworth Press

Printed in Great Britain by
MPG Books Ltd (www.mpg-books.co.uk)

Contents

Picture Acknowledgements

All line drawings are by **Dianne Breeze**, with the exception of those on pages 53 and 77, which are by **Carole Vincer**.

Picture sources
The author and publishers wish to acknowledge the following books as sources for some of the illustrations:

- **The BHS Manual of Equitation**, Consultant Editor Islay Auty FBHS, published by Kenilworth Press

- **The BHS Complete Manual of Stable Management**, Consultant Editor Islay Auty FBHS, published by Kenilworth Press

- **The BHS Veterinary Manual**, by P. Stewart Hastie MRCVS, published by Kenilworth Press

- **Learn to Ride with The British Horse Society**, by Islay Auty FBHS, published by Kenilworth Press

- **Lungeing and Long-Reining**, by Jennie Loriston-Clarke FBHS, published by Kenilworth Press

- **Threshold Picture Guide No. 8, Field Management**, by Mary Gordon Watson, published by Kenilworth Press

- **Threshold Picture Guide No. 43, Functional Anatomy**, by Dr Chris Colles BVetMed, PhD, MRCVS, published by Kenilworth Press

How to Use This Book

THE AIM OF THIS BOOK is to provide students working towards Stage 2, with detailed guidance to help prepare thoroughly for the examination. The information is laid out as follows:

The individual **elements** of each subject that you will be tested on are listed under a broad category heading, e.g. Grooming, Clothing, etc.

Each topic has a section on '**What the examiner is looking for**', which breaks down the subject matter of each 'element', giving a fuller picture of the level of information required or what you might be asked to do. As each topic is discussed the relevant element to which it applies is given in brackets.

The sections entitled '**How to become competent**' guide you as to where you might be able to access the knowledge or practical application.

Throughout, the book is aiming to clearly outline the requirements of the syllabus, but you are still encouraged to go and find out the knowledge required for each subject for yourself. This ensures that you have taken the time and trouble to consolidate your 'book learning' with the true practical application that is so integral to the care and management of horses.

The sections on gaining competence should be sufficiently flexible for you to be able to adapt the requirements to your own situation with horses. Whatever that situation may be, you must demonstrate a certain speed and efficiency which would be appropriate to your competence for working in the industry and maintaining credibility at Stage 2 level.

A Stage 2 worker should be capable of looking after stabled horses and those at grass, with competence and efficiency within a relevant timescale appropriate to the experience at this level. As a Stage 2 worker you should be capable of independent, self-motivated work on a day-to-day basis, but there should always be a more senior member of staff to whom you can turn for advice if necessary, or in the event of an emergency.

Understanding the Stage 2 Exam

After Stage 1

You will have achieved BHS Stage 1 through one of two routes: either you worked steadily through levels 1–6 of the Society's Progressive Riding Tests (PRTs) in your regular lessons at a BHS-Approved Riding Establishment; or you chose to sit the BHS Stage 1 examination and were successful in passing the Horse Knowledge and Care section and the Riding section, which combine to give you the BHS Stage 1 certificate. Whichever of these pathways you chose, you are now in a position to consider aiming for BHS Stage 2.

When working toward an examination, whatever the standard or subject, it is essential to consolidate the knowledge required at that level. This gives you confidence and assurance in your skills, which in turn promotes motivation to seek further ability and competence at a higher level.

Think in terms of developing experience and ability alongside further training, gradually moving yourself toward the expertise required at the next level of examination. You should then be capable of taking and passing the Stage 2 exam.

Requirements of Stage 2

The candidate must hold either BHS Stage 1 or the Progressive Riding Tests 1–6 inclusive as a prerequisite for applying to take Stage 2.

The candidate must understand the general management and requirements of horses for their health and well-being. Working under regular but not constant supervision, the candidate should be able to carry out the care of stabled and grass-kept horses during all seasons of the year. He/she must have an understanding of how the horse adjusts his balance to carry a rider. The candidate must be capable of riding a quiet, experienced horse or pony in the countryside and on the public highway as well as in a manège, or indoor school.

- It is possible to study for and achieve Stage 2 if you are a committed amateur rider who spends a lot of time around horses as well as riding several times a week.

- It is also possible to work for Stage 2 if you own your own horse and have some guidance in your riding (perhaps regular lessons or training at Riding Club clinics with an instructor who is either BHS qualified, or who understands the requirements of the BHS Stage exams).

- It is probably easiest to work for Stage 2 if you are in a regular training situation (either at college or a commercial establishment where students are trained for BHS exams).

- Whatever your chosen pathway towards Stage 2, remember that it is a standard that begins to expect a confirmed practical ability in certain tasks of horsemastership and riding, and these can only be achieved by **practice**.

Riding and Road Safety Test

The Riding and Road Safety Certificate is a prerequisite for the riding section of the Stage 2 exam.

The aim of the Riding and Road Safety Test is, in conjunction with the Highway Code, to promote responsible, considerate and courteous riding on the public highway by all riders.

In these days of ever-increasing traffic volumes on the public highway, it is essential that every rider takes responsibility for his or her own safety on the road and maintains courtesy towards and understanding of other road users. The Society's well-respected Riding and Road Safety Test has been taken by thousands of riders and is a tangible way of addressing every rider's safety on the public highways.

If you are on a training course as a full-time student, it is almost certain that those in charge of your training will 'build in' the road safety training and exam in the preparation for your Stage 2.

If you are working for your Stage 2 independently then there are various ways you can find out about the availability and training for Riding and Road Safety Tests in your area. You can contact:

- The Safety Office at The British Horse Society (see page 127 for address) for details of local contacts.

- Your Regional or County Road Safety Officer, who will tell you of courses and tests in your area.

Training can be given by designated trained road-safety instructors, and the BHS publishes a very comprehensive 'Riding and Road Safety Manual'. Called *Riding and Roadcraft*, this book is essential reading for anyone training for the test. The manual should be read in conjunction with a current copy of *The Highway Code*, which has a section specifically dedicated to horses on the road. While it is not compulsory, it is strongly recommended that riders receive a minimum of eight hours tuition from a BHS-Approved Safety Trainer before they undertake the test.

The Test

Divided into three parts.

- The theory test. A multiple-choice question paper.

- The simulated road test. A controlled, simulated test.

- The road test on the public highway. An individual test on the road.

On achievement of the Riding and Road Safety Test, your certificate **MUST** be sent into the Exams Office with your Stage 2 application. If the exam date has been applied for before you take the test, then you **MUST** take the certificate to the Stage 2 exam: the chief examiner will need to see it before allowing you to take the riding section of Stage 2.

Practical Application

Reference has already been made to the practical ability that you must achieve for Stage 2 level. As you read this book and each section is explained, it is vital that you are very familiar with each unit and element. Below are listed ways in which your practical skills may be developed if you are not in a regular 'working with horses' environment.

- Spend **at least** one **full** day a week working in a yard where horses are kept both stabled and at grass.

- Make sure that your work is observed and supervised by someone who can advise you on safe and good practice.

- If you care for your own horse (e.g. DIY livery) try to follow a system of good practice and if possible ask someone to observe some of the tasks you do (e.g. tacking up or grooming) on a regular basis and accept their constructive criticism.

- Spend one day a week in a 'day-release' training situation, where you can undergo training and carry out supervised yard-work practice.

When carrying out any task, being able 'to do it' does not necessarily demonstrate professional competence in an exam situation. It is essential that the way you 'do it' underlines your awareness of good and safe practice, and is a skill that you could transfer to someone else with less competence. By copying you they would develop good practice themselves and not be put at risk by following your example and method.

Your practical application (or tasks) must be:

- Safe.

- In the interests of the horse's welfare.

- Completed efficiently and in a reasonable timescale.

- An acceptable method for someone else to copy or learn from.

There is no substitute for practice. Knowledge of the subject must be thorough and sufficient for the level required, but practical competence is **vital**.

Stage 2
Horse Knowledge and Care

Syllabus

Candidates must be physically fit in order to carry out yard and fieldwork efficiently, without undue stress and strain. They will be expected to demonstrate competent use of time.

Candidates will be expected to give practical demonstrations, as well as be involved in discussion of selected tasks and topics.

> **IMPORTANT**: Candidates are advised to check that they are working from the latest examination syllabus, as examination content and procedure are liable to alteration. Contact the BHS Examinations Office for up-to-date information regarding the syllabus.

BHS Stage 2 (Horse Knowledge and Care) – Syllabus

Candidates must be physically fit in order to carry out yard and fieldwork efficiently without undue stress and strain. They will be expected to demonstrate competent use of time.
Candidates will be expected to give practical demonstrations as well as be involved in discussion of selected tasks and topics.

Unit code number S2CARE

Learning Outcomes	Element	Assessment criteria	
The candidate should be able to:		The candidate has achieved this outcome because s/he can:	Influence
Grooming	1.1.1	Outline a variety of grooming methods including strapping	Supporting
	1.1.2	Demonstrate safe efficient grooming procedures	Compulsory
Know how to strap, quarter and care for the horse after exercise. Plait manes and tails.	1.2.1	Demonstrate competent use of time	Compulsory
	1.2.2	Show efficient working pace	Compulsory
	1.3.1	Explain the importance of after-work care	Supporting
	1.4.1	Demonstrate plaiting routines for the mane	Compulsory
	1.4.2	Demonstrate plaiting routines for the tail	Supporting
Clothing	2.1.1	Identify a variety of rugs in common use	Supporting
	2.1.2	Demonstrate safe efficient rug and blanket fitting	Compulsory
Know how to; fit blankets and various types of rugs. Bandage for warmth and protection.	2.2.1	Demonstrate safe efficient methods of applying stable bandages	Compulsory
	2.2.2	Demonstrate correct travel bandaging	Supporting
Wash and store rugs. Prepare a horse for travelling.	2.3.1	Apply and fit appropriate equipment used for travelling (rugs etc)	Compulsory
	2.3.2	Apply and fit travelling boots	Compulsory
	2.4.1	Show efficient procedures throughout	Compulsory
	2.5.1	Give suitable washing and storing methods	Supporting
Saddlery	3.1.1	Identify ill fitting and inappropriate tack	Compulsory
	3.1.2	Explain the consequences of using ill fitting tack	Supporting
Know:	3.2.1	Demonstrate safe efficient fitting of tack for riding	Compulsory
The basic principles of fitting tack in everyday use. The cleaning and care of all saddlery. The inspecting of horses for injury from ill-fitting saddles, bridles, boots, etc.	3.2.2	Demonstrate safe efficient fitting of tack for lungeing	Compulsory
	3.3.1	Apply a variety of boots used for protection, found in everyday use	Compulsory
	3.4.1	Show effective fitting of breastplates and or martingales	Compulsory
	3.5.1	Describe how to clean and care for saddlery to be stored	Supporting
Handling	4.1.1	Identify possibilities of risk and discomfort to self, the horse and others when working in stables	Supporting
Know and demonstrate safe, efficient procedures when efficiently carrying out practical work.	4.2.1	Apply safe procedures for self, the horse and others	Compulsory
	4.3.1	Show effective safe methods of working to maintain control and confidence in the horse	Supporting
	4.4.1	Demonstrate efficient use of time	Compulsory
Lungeing	5.1.1	Show safe control of the horse	Compulsory
	5.2.1	Demonstrate appropriate work for exercise	Supporting
Know how to lunge a horse for exercise. Side reins may or may not be used.	5.3.1	Apply safe efficient handling of the equipment	Compulsory
	5.4.1	Show an effective lungeing method	Compulsory
	5.5.1	Discuss safe efficient lungeing procedures	Supporting
	5.6.1	Explain principles of rhythm and balance	Supporting
Stable Design	6.1.1	Outline appropriate stable dimensions for horses and ponies	Compulsory
Know:	6.2.1	Give suitable materials for stable construction	Supporting
The basic requirements of size and safe construction of a stable and its fittings.	6.3.1	Describe the importance of good ventilation and how this may be provided	Compulsory
	6.4.1	Define the importance of good drainage	Supporting
	6.5.1	Give minimum doorway widths	Supporting
	6.6.1	Describe essential stable fittings and their use	Supporting

Stage 2 – Horse Knowledge & Care

Unit code number S2CARE			
Learning Outcomes	Element	Assessment criteria	Influence
The candidate should be able to:		The candidate has achieved this outcome because s/he can:	
Shoeing Know: The farrier's tools and their function, how to remove shoes in an emergency and the reasons for regular foot attention.	7.1.1	Give the farrier's shoeing procedure	Compulsory
	7.2.1	Outline the farrier's tools and their uses	Compulsory
	7.3.1	Show how to remove a twisted shoe	Supporting
	7.3.2	Demonstrate effective handling of the horse and tools	Supporting
	7.4.1	Describe problems experienced when shoes are left on too long	Compulsory
	7.5.1	Explain the importance of regular trimming of unshod hooves	Supporting
Clipping & Trimming Know: The underlying purposes of clipping and trimming. Essential safety measures and procedures. How to maintain clippers in good order. Know when and how to trim.	8.1.1	Demonstrate pulling of manes and tails	Compulsory
	8.1.2	Explain when and when not to pull and trim horses and ponies	Supporting
	8.1.3	Explain trimming using scissors, comb or clippers	Supporting
	8.2.1	Outline the reasons for clipping and frequency of clipping	Supporting
	8.3.1	Give a variety of different clips and their purpose	Compulsory
	8.4.1	Show and/or describe the maintenance checks to clippers made before, during and after use	Supporting
	8.4.2	Describe how to maintain clipper machines	Supporting
	8.5.1	Explain safety aspects for self, horse and handler	Compulsory
Anatomy and Physiology Know: The signs of health and ill-health. The equine skeletal frame, the position of the horse's main internal organs. A basic understanding of the horse's digestive system, and the structure and function of the horse's foot.	9.1.1	Outline the general health and condition of the horse in front of you	Compulsory
	9.2.1	Outline the horse's digestive system and basic function of individual parts	Supporting
	9.3.1	Identify the horse's main internal organs	Compulsory
	9.4.1	Describe why bulk is important to the horse's digestive system	Supporting
	9.5.1	Give the function of bacteria found in the hind-gut	Supporting
	9.6.1	Identify the parts of the skeleton on the horse in-front of you	Compulsory
	9.7.1	Give the principles of horse health	Supporting
	9.8.1	Give the horse's normal temperature, pulse, and respiration rates	Supporting
	9.9.1	Describe how breathing, can be an indication of health or ill health	Supporting
	9.9.2	Describe how eating, can be an indication of health or ill health	Supporting
	9.9.3	Describe how droppings, can each be an indication of health or ill health	Supporting
	9.9.4	Describe how posture, can be an indication of health or ill health	Compulsory
	9.10.1	Describe the external parts of the horse's foot	Compulsory
	9.10.2	Explain the function of the frog	Supporting
	9.10.3	Explain the importance of the white line	Supporting
Horse Behaviour Know: The value of calmness and kindness in establishing the horse's confidence and improving his well-being and therefore his work.	10.1.1	Give examples of possible causes of unsettled behaviour in horses at grass during summer months	Supporting
	10.2.1	Give examples of how by stabling the horse we go against his natural lifestyle	Compulsory
	10.3.1	Describe the indications of nervousness in the horse in a variety of situations	Compulsory
	10.4.1	Describe safe methods of handling horses in a variety of situations	Supporting
	10.5.1	Give examples of good yard practice when accommodating a new horse	Supporting
	10.6.1	Describe why a normally stable kept horse may be difficult to catch when he is out in a field	Supporting
	10.7.1	Give reasons for anti-social behaviour in the horse when he is ridden in company	Supporting
	10.8.1	Describe how the horse might behave if the tack doesn't fit	Compulsory

Unit code number S2CARE			
Learning Outcomes	**Element**	**Assessment criteria**	
			Influence
The candidate should be able to:		The candidate has achieved this outcome because s/he can:	
Horse Health	11.1.1	Describe the symptoms of unsoundness in the horse	Supporting
	11.2.1	Describe the treatments for a variety of minor wounds	Compulsory
Know when a horse is off colour or is not sound enough to be worked.	11.3.1	Give the rules of basic sick nursing	Compulsory
	11.4.1	Give the indications that would necessitate a visit from the vet	Compulsory
Know the treatment of minor wounds and basic nursing and when to call the veterinary surgeon. Know the importance of regular worming.	11.5.1	Give a list of essential basic equine health records	Supporting
	11.6.1	Describe the indications of worm infestation in the horse	Supporting
	11.6.2	Give an appropriate worm control programme for the horse	Compulsory
	11.7.1	Give the signs of a horse having problems with its teeth	Supporting
Fittening	12.1.1	Give an appropriate fittening programme for use when bringing a horse up from grass and into regular work.	Compulsory
Know how to relate condition, feeding and progressive exercise when bringing a horse up from resting at grass into regular work.	12.2.1	Give the possible causes of coughs and colds when first bringing a horse up from grass	Compulsory
	12.2.2	Give the possible causes of saddle and girth galls when first bringing a horse up from grass	Compulsory
	12.2.3	Give the potential consequences of dust and/or diet change when first bringing a horse up from grass	Compulsory
Know the process of cooling off after work and roughing off a fit horse.	12.3.1	Give examples of feeding in relation to the fittening programme and condition of the horse when bringing up from grass and into regular work	Compulsory
Regular work: six hours per week at walk, trot and canter without stressing (refer to Examinations Handbook)	12.4.1	Give a suitable programme for roughing off a fit horse.	Compulsory
	12.5.1	Show awareness of the possible causes of concussion injuries when riding out	Supporting
	12.5.2	Show awareness of the possible causes of strain injuries when riding out	Supporting
	12.6.1	Give the procedure for cooling the horse off after work	Supporting
	12.6.2	Outline care of the horse after work	Supporting
General Knowledge	13.1.1	Describe safe procedures when riding on the highway	Compulsory
	13.1.2	Describe your procedure when riding onto or turning off a major road	Compulsory
Know: The Country Code, safety measures and correct procedures when riding on the public highway. The correct procedures in the event of an accident.	13.1.3	List high visibility equipment suitable for use when riding on the roads	Compulsory
	13.2.1	Give examples of good behaviour when riding on bridleways	Compulsory
Know the aims and structure of The British Horse Society and the benefits of membership.			
	13.2.2	Give examples of correct action when meeting others on tracks and bridleways.	Supporting
	13.3.1	List the aims of the British Horse Society	Supporting
	13.3.2	List the departments in the British Horse Society	Supporting
	13.4.1	Describe the action to be taken in the event of an accident on your yard	Compulsory
Grassland Care	14.1.1	Describe the ideal field that would be suitable for horses	Compulsory
	14.2.1	Give examples of good practice when maintaining good quality grazing	Supporting
Have basic knowledge of good pasture and its maintenance. Know plants which are poisonous to horses.	14.3.1	Describe common poisonous plants that may be found in and around grazing land	Compulsory

Unit code number S2CARE			
Learning Outcomes	Element	Assessment criteria	Influence
The candidate should be able to:		The candidate has achieved this outcome because s/he can:	
Watering and Feeding	15.1.1	Give the rules of watering	Compulsory
	15.1.2	Give examples of a variety of watering systems and their advantages/ disadvantages	Supporting
Know the advantages and disadvantages of various watering systems and the importance of water to the horse.	15.2.1	Give the rules of feeding and describe their importance	Compulsory
	15.3.1	Assess the quality of a variety of feed samples	Supporting
	15.4.1	Give examples of feedstuffs that have a heating effect	Supporting
	15.4.2	Give examples of feedstuffs that have a fattening effect	Supporting
Know a variety of common feed stuffs and their respective values.	15.4.3	Give examples of feedstuffs that are suitable for horses doing fast work	Supporting
Have a practical knowledge of how to prepare specific feedstuffs.	15.5.1	Give a suitable supplementary diet for a horse/ pony living at grass during the winter	Compulsory
	15.6.1	Give examples of suitable feed for old horses	Supporting
Know the basic principles of feeding old, or sick horses, and horses and ponies at grass in all seasons.	15.6.2	Give examples of suitable feed for sick horses	Supporting
	15.7.1	Describe how to prepare sugar beet for feeding	Compulsory
	15.7.2	Describe how to prepare a bran mash	Supporting
	15.7.3	Give the reasons for feeding soaked hay	Supporting
	15.7.4	Describe how to prepare soaked hay	Supporting
Know how to make a simple feed chart.	15.8.1	Name and describe an alternative to hay in the horse's diet	Compulsory
	15.9.1	Describe how to make a feed chart	Compulsory

If you have recently read the BHS Training Manual for Stage 1, or you have taken the Stage 1 exam within the last twelve months, you will already be familiar with the format of the syllabus (which changed in 2003). For those of you who have not seen the syllabus in this format before, a little explanation will reassure you that the standard and requirements of Stage 2 are unchanged. The syllabus is clearly divided into Elements broadly covering individual topics (e.g. grooming), and then sections within each element break down the expected knowledge and understanding. Within this book the following symbols are used:

C = COMPULSORY

S = SUPPORTING

Compulsory elements appear in the practical and theoretical parts of your exam. It is likely that most, if not all , compulsory elements of the syllabus will be examined during your Stage 2. As the name suggests, the supporting elements add depth and weight to the demonstration of competence that should be shown in the compulsory elements.

Make sure that you are confident and competent in all areas of the compulsory requirements. Make sure that you feel comfortable with all the supporting elements – there should be nothing within the syllabus that you have never heard of!

All work that was required at Stage 1 should now be seen to be carried out to a higher standard of efficiency. Candidates should show an increasing awareness of the needs of the horse(s) in their care and the importance of co-operating and communicating with fellow workers. In addition candidates will be expected to show knowledge and practical ability in the subjects that follow.

Grooming

Know:

How to strap, quarter and care for the horse after exercise.

Plaiting manes and tails.

ELEMENT

S	**1.1.1**	Outline a variety of grooming methods including strapping.
C	**1.1.2**	Demonstrate safe, efficient grooming methods/procedures.
C	**1.2.1**	Demonstrate competent use of time.
C	**1.2.2**	Show efficient working pace.
S	**1.3.1**	Explain the importance of after-work care.
C	**1.4.1**	Demonstrate plaiting routines for the mane.
S	**1.4.2**	Demonstrate plaiting routines for the tail.

What the examiner will look for

- You are likely to be asked to demonstrate your system of grooming a horse thoroughly. (Elements 1.1.1 and 1.1.2) (You may be asked to describe 'quartering', 'brushing off after work', full groom and 'strapping'.) Be sure that you can discuss fully the knowledge behind each of these terms, and that you are able to show a vigorous ability to groom the horse with the body brush and curry comb. Strapping refers to the 'wisping' or 'banging' of the muscular areas of the horse's body, which helps to stimulate circulation and muscle tone in the fit horse. Strapping can also refer to the complete grooming procedure which includes wisping.

- You should not only demonstrate competence but show through discussion your understanding of safe practice, positioning yourself and/or the horse in such a way that injury is minimised when grooming the face, hind legs and picking up feet. (Element 1.1.2)

- Throughout your grooming work you should demonstrate an awareness of the horse's reaction and manner to you (e.g. you must recognise if he is tickly in sensitive areas and threatens to nip or kick; similarly when strapping you should be aware of the horse's acceptance of the treatment).

- You should be aware of how much time it would be practical to allocate each horse if you were responsible for more than one. You should be able to estimate that it might take 5 minutes to quarter in the morning, 30 to 40 minutes for a full groom and strapping, and another 5 to 15 minutes to make the horse comfortable after work. (Element 1.3.1)

- Knowledge of how the after-work care might vary according to weather conditions (a wet or muddy horse) or how hard the horse had worked (washing off a sweaty horse) would be expected. (Element 1.3.1)

- Efficient use of time is essential if you are responsible for more than one horse and this also demonstrates your competence. (Elements 1.2.1 and 1.2.2) If asked to groom, try to forget the examiner and 'get on with the job' as if you really had to turn the horse out immaculately for your employer.

- You are likely to be asked to put in one or two plaits in a mane. (Element 1.4.1) This is most likely to be with a needle and thread, so make sure that you are proficient. If you are a little nervous, a fiddly job like plaiting can be difficult if you are not totally familiar with the task in normal circumstances. The mane may be too short/long/thick/thin. Be prepared to discuss the condition of the mane and how easy it is to manage.

Plaiting a mane, and securing with needle and thread.

Plaiting a tail.

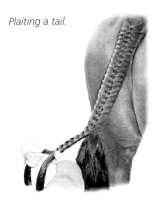

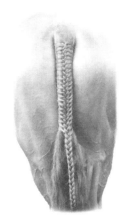

completing the end of the plait   stitching to secure   finished tail

- You may be asked to plait a tail. (Element 1.4.2) You must be able to do this. So if this is something you cannot yet do, ask someone to show you how and then practice thoroughly before your exam.

How to become competent

- In any establishment there are **always** horses who will benefit from a little extra time spent on grooming them.

- Unless there are several horses that you are responsible for on a daily basis, then you must go out of your way to practise grooming procedure and work on your system, efficiency and timing.

- Ask your instructor, or preferably someone who is either a BHS examiner or a Pony Club examiner, to watch you groom and to ask you questions. Accept constructive criticism and work to be more proficient.

- Make sure that you are able to explain clearly the theory behind good grooming.

- Make sure that you can demonstrate and explain the following: quartering; brushing off after work; strapping; grooming the face; grooming (finger-combing) the tail; spongeing the eyes, nose and dock; plaiting a mane and tail in full (with thread).

- Be fully aware of the reasons for the after-care of the horse when he has worked.

Clothing

How to fit blankets and various types of rugs.

Bandage for warmth and protection.

Wash and store rugs.

Prepare a horse for travelling.

ELEMENT

S	**2.1.1**	Identify a variety of rugs in common use.
C	**2.1.2**	Demonstrate safe, efficient rug and blanket fitting.
C	**2.2.1**	Demonstrate the safe, efficient method of applying stable bandages.
S	**2.2.2**	Demonstrate correct travel bandaging.
C	**2.3.1**	Apply and fit appropriate equipment used for travelling (rugs etc.)
C	**2.3.2**	Apply and fit travelling boots.
C	**2.4.1**	Show efficient procedures throughout.
S	**2.5.1**	Give suitable washing and storing methods.

What the examiner is looking for

- By this stage, you should have come across a variety of rugs in your day-to-day care of horses over the seasons of the year. (Element 2.1.1) These should include rugs worn at night in the stable (winter and summer, with knowledge as to the difference); rugs used for turnout; rugs used for fly protection; anti-sweat rugs; and rugs for travelling in different weather conditions. The more types of rugs you have encountered, the better.

- Your ability to choose the rug, or rugs, which are most appropriate to the weather conditions of the day or the conditions in which a horse might have to travel (e.g. lorry or trailer).

■ When handling horses that you know well, it is easy to become complacent about how you manage them. It is, however, essential when dealing with an unfamiliar or young horse, that you adopt a procedure for fitting equipment that is safe for both you and the horse, in the event that he behaves unpredictably. (Elements 2.1.2, 2.2.1 and 2.4.1) Whereas at home, with your own horse, it would be quite acceptable to throw a rug over his back, this would not be wise with a horse that is unfamiliar to you. The examiner will expect you to demonstrate a procedure for applying rugs to a horse that is unfamiliar to you (even if you are taking the exam at a centre where you know the horses well). (Element 2.1.2) With this in mind, fold rugs and blankets and place them across the withers, then unfold them over the horse's back.

■ Throughout the fitting of horse clothing you will be expected to discuss whether the item does or does not fit the horse. If the fit is inappropriate it is important that you can recognise this and identify it . For example, is the rug too long over the tail/too short/tight around the shoulders/too short or long?

■ Be familiar with the fitting of bandages for travel and for wear in the stable. (Elements 2.2.1 and 2.2.2) Be able to discuss types of bandage materials used and the types of padding or protection that might be used underneath the bandages. Be able to talk about the different jobs that each type of bandage is employed to do for the horse (e.g. stable bandages for warmth, travel bandages for protection).

■ Be able to fit travelling boots. (Element 2.3.2)

Stable bandage – padding just below the bandage, to prevent unnecessary interference with bedding

Travel bandage – more padding for protection, and padding lower to protect coronary band

- Throughout the fitting of all the clothing you must demonstrate a safe procedure for both your own and the horse's welfare. (Element 2.4.1.) You must be sufficiently competent at the tasks to show a relevant speed for completion appropriate to the level (i.e. someone at Stage 2 level would be quicker than someone of Stage 1 ability).

- You may be asked about conditions for storing and caring for rugs and clothing in general. (Element 2.5.1) You should be conversant with methods of storing rugs when not in use (e.g. out-of-season winter rugs). Be aware of the need for repair of damaged rugs, reproofing of outdoor rugs, and the washing and safe storage of all such equipment.

How to become competent

- Handle horses in as many different types of yard as you can. In this way you are likely to see horses wearing a variety of rugs for different weathers and appropriate to different after-work conditions.

- Make sure that you regularly apply rugs and remove them following a safe and efficient system. (You may throw rugs onto a familiar horse, but practice until you are completely competent at folding rugs and applying them as if to a nervous or unknown horse.)

Horse dressed to travel, with poll guard, rug appropriate to weather conditions, tail bandage and tail guard, and travelling boots for leg protection.

- Ask your instructor to supervise and monitor regularly your application of rugs and bandages.

- By working around horses in different weather conditions and seeing horses travel to competitions you will develop an awareness of which type of rug to choose for any situation.

- If a horse in your yard needs to wear stable bandages or is travelling regularly, ask if you can put on his equipment. If this is not possible then find the equipment and practise with it often so that you are familiar and efficient with the task. Remember that in an exam you may be nervous, which can lower your proficiency.

- Observe other, more experienced people apply rugs and bandages. It can be very motivating to watch someone who is quick and efficient. Your aim should be to emulate their competence.

Saddlery

Know:

The basic principles of fitting tack in everyday use.

The cleaning and care of all saddlery.

The inspecting of horses for injury from ill-fitting saddles, bridles, boots, etc.

ELEMENT

C	**3.1.1**	Identify ill-fitting and inappropriate tack.
S	**3.1.2**	Explain the consequences of using ill-fitting tack.
C	**3.2.1**	Demonstrate safe, efficient tack-fitting for riding.
C	**3.2.2**	Demonstrate safe, efficient fitting of tack for lungeing.
C	**3.3.1**	Apply a variety of boots used for protection, found in everyday use.
C	**3.4.1**	Show effective fitting of breastplates and or martingales.
S	**3.5.1**	Describe how to clean and care for saddlery to be stored.

What the examiner is looking for

- You must be able to recognise ill-fitting tack, and tack which is not appropriate to the horse, for whatever reason. Examples would be: a pinching browband or one which is too small; a noseband which is rubbing against a cheek bone, or a bit which is incorrectly fitted, causing friction in the mouth. Inappropriate tack might include saddlery in need of repair and numnahs or girths which need washing. (Element 3.1.1)

- You must understand and be able to describe the consequences of using ill-fitting tack. (Element 3.1.2) These include the risk of injury and discomfort to the horse, both of which may result in an accident to the rider.

- You will be required to fit tack for everyday use and also prepare a horse for lungeing (a rider). This will include fitting a lunge cavesson and side-reins. (Elements 3.2.1 and 3.2.2) Your tack fitting must be efficient and workmanlike. It must have due regard for the safety of the horse and the equipment (e.g. do not leave the stable door open with the horse loose while you tack up; don't leave the saddle on the stable door where the horse may push it off).

- Your tack fitting must be systematic and thorough, so that it leaves the horse safely equipped for its rider. For example, when fitting the bridle, check the fit of browband, the fit of throatlatch, the position and tightness of the noseband, and the position and width of the bit.

- You will be expected to choose and apply some boots which might be used for lungeing the horse or for everyday use. (Element 3.3.1)

- You will be asked to put on some type of breastplate and/or a martingale. The martingale will either be a running or standing type, so be familiar with both. (Element 3.4.1)

- You will be asked to talk about the maintenance of tack, including everyday care to the seasonal treatment of rugs and other equipment, which needs to be safely stored for the winter or summer off-season. (Element 3.5.1)

How to become competent

- In your working situation you should be applying tack on a daily basis to the horses you look after. Make frequent checks that the tack is sitting comfortably on

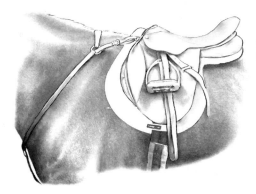

General-purpose saddle fitted with numnah and breastplate.

Running martingale.

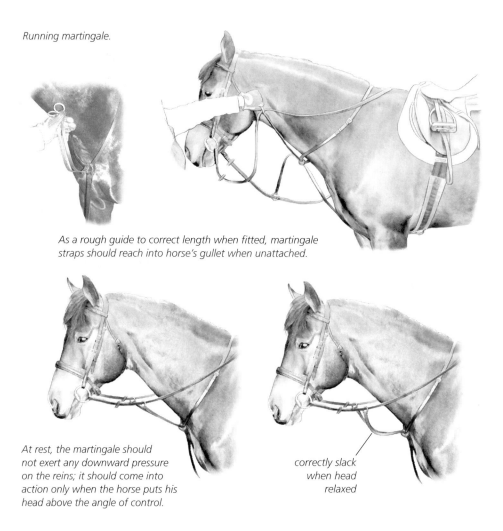

As a rough guide to correct length when fitted, martingale
straps should reach into horse's gullet when unattached.

At rest, the martingale should
not exert any downward pressure
on the reins; it should come into
action only when the horse puts his
head above the angle of control.

correctly slack
when head
relaxed

the horse. It is easy to become complacent with tack that you know and use regularly.

■ Try to apply tack to horses that you are less familiar with, and handle the tack with a more inquisitive approach. Look at the condition of the leather and consider its maintenance – do you think it is supple and well cared for?

From time to time try to fit tack to horses using items that will not automatically fit. Undo all the keepers and practise measuring the bridle against the horse's head to estimate fit. Remember, once you are happy with the fit, then replace all the keepers so that the bridle is fitted neatly and tidily.

- Learn to look at saddles with a view to judging whether the saddle looks too big or too small on the horse's back.

- Ask your instructor to show you clearly how to assess saddle fit, including the clearance over the wither, the fit on the shoulders, the room along the spine, and the length and depth of the saddle.

- Whenever you see other horses (not those you know), look at the type of boots they are wearing and consider the type of work they might be doing in those particular boots. (At a show jumping competition, for example, you may see a lot of open-fronted tendon boots, whereas at a dressage show you will see far more schooling boots, usually white.)

- Look in your local tack shops at the wide variety of boots now available. Most boots will say on them what specific job they are designed for.

- Make sure that you have fitted boots as often as possible.

- Practise the fitting and basic use of side-reins for lungeing. You must be able to apply side-reins for lungeing a rider.

- Side-reins can be fitted in different ways, but the most common method would be to slip the rein around the rear girth strap and under the front girth strap, above the buckle guard, if there is one and there is room. Side-reins should be adjusted initially to be the same length on both sides.

- Learning to correctly fit a lungeing cavesson needs some guidance. Lunge cavessons are specialist pieces of equipment and must fit snugly around the nose so that the attachment of the rein on the nose is comfortable. Correct fitting of the strap around the jowl or cheek is also important to ensure that the cavesson does not slide around and interfere with the horse's eye on either side. It is usually safer to apply the lunge cavesson immediately before the horse is taken from his stable. An unattended horse left tied up while wearing a lunge cavesson could become entangled or injured by the equipment.

- If the horse is to be ridden it is usually preferable (but not essential) to put the cavesson under the bridle and remove the noseband from the bridle.

- The more experience you have of applying various types of boots and saddlery, the easier it will be in your exam when there is a wide range of equipment available and you must choose items to fit to a specific horse.

■ Make sure that you have had lots of practice in the day-to-day care and cleaning of tack, so that you can easily recognise tack in supple and good condition and that which is dry, hard and neglected.

■ Try to have used a range of cleaning products, such as bar saddle soap, neatsfoot oil and a heavy-duty leather dressing such as kaocholine.

■ Be aware of how you maintain tack that is thoroughly wet and muddy, new tack, and neglected dry tack.

■ Notice how boots are cleaned and maintained in your yard. Get involved in this procedure, even if you are not a full-time worker in the establishment.

■ Whenever you get the opportunity, discuss the tack that is used at your establishment: find out what is used when and why. Watch others who are more experienced than you fit equipment. Ask questions about anything you have not seen or experienced before.

■ Hands-on practice and observation of others using various pieces of equipment builds competence.

Handling

Safe, efficient procedures when efficiently carrying out practical work.

ELEMENT

S   **4.1.1** Identify possibilities of risk and discomfort to self, the horse and others when working in stables.

C   **4.2.1** Apply safe procedures for self, the horse and others.

S   **4.3.1** Show effective, safe methods of working when maintaining control and confidence in the horse.

C   **4.4.1** Demonstrate efficient use of time.

What the examiner is looking for

- Anyone involved in any aspect of riding or caring for horses should recognise that the very nature of the activity conveys a degree of risk. This is not only because the horse is an animal but also because he is a big animal, which, mismanaged or handled badly, could cause injury. (Element 4.1.1)

- Anyone working in and around horses will identify a wide range of 'risks' in the stable yard and while riding. The most valuable asset that you can develop is **awareness** around the stable yard, particularly in the vicinity of any horse, but especially around those with whom you are unfamiliar. (Element 4.1.1)

- You must be able to describe or list some of the risks, minor and major, to you and the horse in and around stables. These would include dangers such as being trodden on by a horse, a horse tripping over equipment left in the yard (wheelbarrow or fork) and injuring himself, a rope burn from a horse pulling away from you if not wearing gloves – the list is endless!

- You must demonstrate procedures which safeguard you and the horse in every situation. (Element 4.2.1) For example, a safe procedure for mucking out a horse would be:

Mucking out in a safe environment. Horse tied up and all equipment that is not in use is safely outside the door.

- • tie the horse up (or remove him if it is practical to do so);

- • gather all necessary equipment and keep it tidily outside the stable door;

- • keep the equipment outside the stable unless you are actually using it;

- • stay aware of the horse and his reactions at all times;

- • on completing the task, untie the horse and safely bolt the stable door, removing all equipment to its appropriate and original place.

■ The safety element, whether for the protection of yourself or the horse, of every procedure that you use must be clearly evident – e.g. the wearing of gloves when turning a horse out safeguards against the risk of a horse pulling away from you and giving you a rope burn on unprotected hands.

■ The methods you adopt in handling horses must demonstrate practical competence, and where necessary would show that you were able to give confidence to a horse while still maintaining control. (Element 4.3.1) For example, if a horse is being strong and unruly, it may be necessary to wrap the lead rope through the noseband of the headcollar and over his nose to give added control; it may even be necessary to put a bridle on him; and in extreme cases use a device such as a Chifney to insist on obedience. Your knowledge and competence must be evident in this respect, but also your ability to soothe and reward the horse when he is brought under control and is obedient.

- Efficient use of time will be required on many occasions throughout this and other levels of competence. Quite simply, efficient use of time in any aspect of practical work demonstrates your familiarity with the task through frequent practice. 'Practice makes perfect' may be a well-worn saying but it is nevertheless appropriate. The only way you will develop efficiency in using your time is through plenty of practical application. (Element 4.4.1)

How to become competent

- The more you work in the stable yard and the more practice you have in handling stabled horses and those kept at grass, the better.

- Discuss with your yard manager or your instructor the areas covered by the Health and Safety policy of the establishment and also the risk assessment procedure.

- If you are a full-time student then these areas should have already been introduced to you. The yard should have certain procedures in place which are there for your safety and that of the horses. Make sure that you follow these policies, and if you are not sure **why** they are there, then ask.

- Inevitably you will learn by experience (we all do). It is hoped that the experiences you have will not be too painful nor in any way inhibiting. For example, no one who has worked for any length of time with horses can say they have never been trodden on; however, once you have been trodden on (and it does hurt) then you are **much** more careful about your proximity to the horse's feet **and** you realise why sturdy shoes or boots are important.

- Break down all the tasks and activities that you do with horses and think of all the areas of risk that are involved with those tasks. If you do this task by task (with some help from your instructor if not a full-time student) then you will build up a comprehensive list of the areas where your awareness needs to be strong and increased. For example, in icy weather the yard is likely to be more slippery. Therefore be careful to pour water carefully into drains; do not allow water to spill – and freeze – on the yard; sprinkle salt or sand on the yard to reduce slip; wear ridged soled shoes to assist in grip; lead horses with added care.

Lungeing

How to lunge a horse for exercise. Side-reins may or may not be used.

ELEMENT

| C | **5.1.1** Show safe control of the horse. |

| S | **5.2.1** Demonstrate appropriate work for exercise. |

| C | **5.3.1** Apply safe, efficient handling of the equipment. |

| C | **5.4.1** Show an effective lungeing method. |

| S | **5.5.1** Discuss safe, efficient lungeing procedures. |

| S | **5.6.1** Explain principles of rhythm and balance. |

What the examiner is looking for

- You will be required to lunge an established trained horse, one that should be obedient to your basic skills of controlling it on the lunge in walk and trot on both reins. (Element 5.1.1)

- If you choose to canter the horse, that is up to you, but it is not expected at this stage. You should be asked to 'exercise' the horse. (Element 5.2.1) Be prepared to make the horse go forward adequately. Some well-trained, sensible lunge horses can verge on being lazy and may endeavour not to work very hard! If necessary, vary your voice to motivate the horse, and, if you have to, use the whip in an encouraging way (avoid letting it 'crack' in case this disturbs another horse in the school). If really necessary, then give the horse a sharp reminder with the end of the lash on his buttock region to remind him to go forward.

- You should show approximately equal work on both reins with frequent transitions in and out of walk and trot (and canter if you feel confident and it helps to make the horse more forward).(Elements 5.2.1 and 5.4.1)

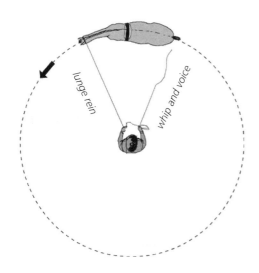

Good positioning of lunger in relation to the horse. handler in centre of circle; horse 'held' in a triangle between the lunge rein and the handler's whip and voice.

lunge rein

whip and voice

- Your handling of the equipment should show a clear system of basic competence. (Element 5.3.1) Make sure that throughout the lungeing session you handle the rein and whip in such a way that it does not inconvenience either you or the horse, that it assists you in carrying out the lunge work competently, and is consistent – for example, make sure the rein is not twisted, and that you have control of the whip, particularly through the changes of rein.

- After the session, the examiner is likely to ask you to comment on the aspects of the lungeing that you were happy/less happy about. Here you may refer to the rhythm and balance of the horse, showing some understanding of these requirements. (Element 5.6.1) You may also discuss where you might lunge a horse if you had no outdoor/indoor school to use. (Element 5.5.1) You may be asked about the use of side-reins (Elements 5.5.1 and 5.3.1) and what affects the length of time you would choose for a lunge session for a horse being exercised.

How to become competent

- You must practise! Lungeing is not something you can learn to do competently unless you practise as much as possible.

- Your training should give you the basic system by which you:

    1. Fold the rein in your hand and manage it without twists.

Safe management of lunge equipment. Reins held in both or one hand, with elbows bent and thumbs on top (as when riding). Whip held in conjunction with the rein or alone.

2. Manage the whip – as you lead the horse out to work, as you lunge, as you change the rein and as you finish, to lead in.

3. Change the rein.

4. Attach the side-reins.

5. Undo the side-reins at the end of the exercise session.

6. Understand the reason behind all the above procedures.

■ To develop the competence in managing the very long rein, it can help to attach it to a fence, gate or similar fixed object and just get used to letting it out and taking it back up again, until you are completely at ease with the process. It is much more difficult when there is a horse at the end of the rein, so learn to manage the rein competently first.

■ Similarly practise managing the whip, passing it from one hand to the other behind your back so that it does not interfere with the horse. If you manage the lash competently it is not necessary to pick it up every time you change the rein, it should be picked up at the start and end of a session when you are leading the horse in and out to the exercise area.

■ Practise 'using' the whip in an active manner. It must be part of a coordinated procedure in which your voice, body stance and language, along with active movement of the whip as required, maintain the horse's respect for you and therefore your control over him.

- Learn to inject versatility into your voice. The horse will have little respect or obedience for a voice that is a whisper, or one that is very monotonous in tone.

- It is probably wise and good practice to have cantered a horse on the lunge. Although it is unlikely that you would be **asked** to canter a horse in a Stage 2 exam, if you have done it before, then you will be far more confident and competent. And if, in a worst-case scenario, the horse were to canter away on the lunge, or you were asked to include canter in your exercise, or you felt that a canter would help you to get the horse going more forward, you would then be better able to deal with these eventualities.

- Watch other people lungeing horses. It can help you immeasurably when you see people more capable than yourself dealing with the same sort of problems as you (for example, the rein going slack and brushing the floor; dropping the whip; or the rein becoming twisted).

- Remember: it is the overall competence that passes or fails you in the task, not the fact that, say, the rein briefly touched the floor or the whip slipped out of your hand!

- Experiment with different methods of holding the rein. Find the one which suits you best and which you can manage most successfully and efficiently.

- Make sure that you have understood the use of side-reins and how they are attached for lungeing. (See Stable Management Element 3.2.2)

- Understand that the horse must be forward before side-reins are attached, and that they must then be even in length. For this level of exam, the side-reins should already be fitted to suit the horse you will lunge. Your only decision is when to attach them, or whether or not to use them at all.

- If the horse is going forward easily for you, then attach the side reins. These will help to keep the horse straight and give him a connection to work into from his activity. If the horse is 'creeping' around, and not actively forward, then the side-reins will probably not help and may actually further inhibit him from going more forward.

- Practise handling the side-reins so that you can attach them efficiently. You should not appear to fiddle with them for a long time. Once you start to use them, it should not be necessary to undo the side-reins to change the rein; only undo them to finish and lead the horse into the stable. When you undo the side-reins, secure them safely by clipping them back to the 'D' ring on the saddle on either side of the pommel.

- You can never practise lungeing enough.

Stable Design

The basic requirements of size and safe construction of a stable and its fittings.

ELEMENT

C	**6.1.1**	Outline appropriate stable dimensions for horse and ponies.
S	**6.2.1**	Give suitable materials for stable construction.
C	**6.3.1**	Describe the importance of good ventilation and how this may be provided.
S	**6.4.1**	Define the importance of good drainage.
S	**6.5.1**	Give minimum doorway widths.
S	**6.6.1**	Describe essential stable fittings and their use.

What the examiner is looking for

- You are likely to be standing either in the stable yard or in a stable itself when the examiner asks about the structure. (Elements 6.1.1/6.2.1/6.5.1/6.6.1) Against an ideal picture, describe the suitability of the facilities around you.

- Stable sizes vary greatly according to whether they have been custom made (in which case they may vary from around 10ft by 10ft (3m by 3m), which could be suitable for a pony, to 12ft by 14ft (3.6m by 4.2m) or bigger, which would be more appropriate for a horse) or they have been converted from existing farm buildings, in which case they may be much larger (or occasionally smaller!). Consider also the height of the roof from a safety point of view, and from the aspect of warmth retention and ventilation. (Element 6.3.1)

- Be able to discuss materials from which stables may be constructed and their relative benefits and disadvantages, including a basic understanding of comparative costs.

An 'American barn-type' stable yard. Stables open onto a covered yard area with an entrance at one or preferably both ends.

- Have some knowledge of how ventilation is provided. (Element 6.3.1) Ventilation is easier in an open, outside block of stables and may need more consideration in an 'American barn-type' building.

- Be aware of where the drainage might be in the stable you are describing, and if there is no apparent system for drainage, discuss the pros and cons of basic drainage in stables. (Element 6.4.1)

- Stable doors should be wide enough for safe entry and exit of both horse and handler. This necessitates a minimum of 4ft to 4ft 6in (120cm to 135cm). Be able to estimate width and also consider the space available in any corridor outside a stable (particularly for indoor stables) (Element 6.5.1)

- Be able to discuss stable fittings and their benefits. (Element 6.6.1)

How to become competent

- Be observant and ask questions. Study any and every stable yard you have the opportunity to visit, even if it is just two stables in the back garden of a friend's house:

- Look at the materials from which stables are built, particularly in older stable yards where the buildings have stood the test of time.

- Ask how cool the stables are in summer and how warm in winter.

- Look at the flooring under the bedding. See whether there are drains or whether the floor is sloping (to the back or the front?). Is the floor concrete? If so, is it ridged for anti-slip? Are there old-fashioned stable bricks?

- What fittings can you see? Lights, mangers, automatic-water devices, tie rings, racks?

- Look at the doors and windows.

- How does the overall yard layout strike you? Take in all the convenient aspects of the set-up (e.g. consider that an overhang on outside stables keeps an area dry to work in but may also cause drips where it ends!).

- Be observant and inquisitive to everything around you; ask questions as to how efficient the stables are for the care and comfort of the horses.

- Read about stable construction and design.

Shoeing

The farrier's tools and their functions.

How to remove shoes in an emergency, and the reasons for regular foot attention.

ELEMENT

C **7.1.1** Give the farrier's shoeing procedure.

C **7.2.1** Outline the farrier's tools and their uses.

S **7.3.1** Show how to remove a twisted shoe.

S **7.3.2** Demonstrate effective handling of the horse and tools.

C **7.4.1** Describe problems experienced when shoes are left on too long.

S **7.5.1** Explain the importance of regular trimming of un-shod hooves.

What the examiner is looking for:

- You should be able to describe the order and procedure in which the farrier removes the shoes, dresses the horse's foot, and prepares and replaces the new or refit shoes. (Element 7.1.1)

- Know thoroughly the tools that the farrier uses, the order in which they are used and the specific use of each tool. (Element 7.2.1)

- Feel confident that you can demonstrate how you would pick up a front and a hind foot, and can handle the necessary tools to remove a shoe in an emergency. (Elements 7.3.1 and 7.3.2)

- Be able to describe the problems that the horse is likely to experience if the shoes are left on for too long. (Element 7.4.1) This would include the horn overgrowing the shoe, the shoe becoming loose and perhaps causing damage to the foot, and

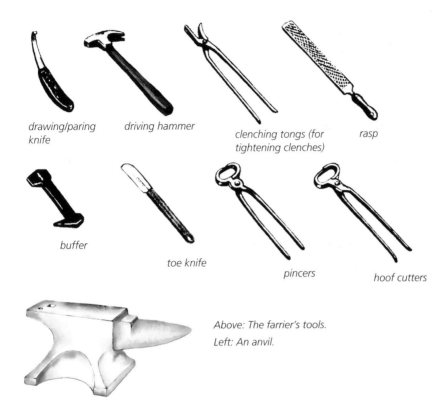

drawing/paring knife

driving hammer

clenching tongs (for tightening clenches)

rasp

buffer

toe knife

pincers

hoof cutters

Above: The farrier's tools.
Left: An anvil.

the balance of the horse's feet being disturbed, which could affect his way of going and soundness.

- Regular trimming of the feet (Element 7.5.1) would prevent all the problems relevant to Element 7.4.1. If the horse is unshod, the feet still need attention – even in spite of natural wear through work, the balance of the feet should be addressed by regular attention and trimming.

How to become competent

- It is absolutely essential that you watch a farrier working as often as you can.

- The more familiar you are with the adept way in which your farrier removes your horse's shoes, the better.

- Familiarise yourself completely with all the tools the farrier uses, know their names and the order in which he uses them.

- You can read up on this subject but also ask questions of your farrier to gain your genuine practical knowledge.

- Make sure that you have handled the tools required to remove a shoe (buffer, driving hammer and pincers).

- Make sure that you regularly practise picking up and holding a front foot and, in turn, a hind foot in such a way that you can use the tools effectively to remove a shoe.

- Ask your farrier (when he is not too busy and in a hurry to get to his next client) if he will let you practise removing a shoe.

- With both a hind and fore foot you need to be able to support the leg and foot in such a way that your hands are free to use the tools to remove the shoe.

- If you watch the farrier you will see exactly how this is done, then you must practise. Make sure you are not wearing your best breeches when doing this as you will ruin them. When you demonstrate this procedure in your exam, pick up a stable rubber (or cloth) and cover your knee to protect your clean breeches. (Farriers wear a leather apron!)

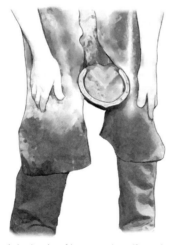

bringing hoof between legs (front foot)

securing leg over one knee (hind foot)

Two methods of securing the foot so that hands are free to remove a shoe.

- In your day-to-day handling of the horse (you should be routinely caring for the feet at least twice a day, picking them out) be observant to the ongoing condition of the feet. If looking at the feet of a new horse make sure that you take careful note of their condition and the state of the shoes.

Clipping and Trimming

The underlying purposes of clipping and trimming. Essential safety measures and procedures. How to maintain clippers in good order.

Know when and how to trim.

ELEMENT

C **8.1.1** Demonstrate pulling of manes and tails.

S **8.1.2** Explain when and when not to pull and trim horses and ponies.

S **8.1.3** Explain trimming, using scissors, comb or clippers.

S **8.2.1** Outline the reasons for clipping and frequency of clipping.

C **8.3.1** Give a variety of different clips and their purpose.

S **8.4.1** Show and/or describe the maintenance checks to clippers, made before, during and after use.

S **8.4.2** Describe how to maintain clipper machines.

C **8.5.1** Explain safety aspects for self, horse and handler.

What the examiner is looking for

- Show an ability to correctly pull a mane and a tail. (Element 8.1.1) This would include showing an understanding that horses vary in their sensitivity to having their manes and tails pulled. You must show the method of back-combing the mane with a small comb, and pulling small amounts of hair from the underside of the mane. When pulling the tail, the hair should be taken primarily from the sides of the tail in the dock region.

- Knowledge of when it is appropriate to pull manes and tails, and trim areas such as heels and ears, would be expected. (Element 8.1.2) Grass-kept animals need

Pulling a mane using a comb.

their manes/tails and feather hair for protection against the weather. Native breeds should be left with full hair as this would be a requirement if they were to be shown in competition.

- You should know that combs are usually used for mane and tail pulling. (Element 8.1.3) There are 'thinning' combs available on the market which reduce the mane and tail hair without actually 'pulling' it. These are useful for more fractious horses that do not like or will not accept having the hair pulled. Clippers may be used on legs and heels of a very heavily feathered horses, but a comb and scissors, well used on the legs and perhaps around the chin and jaw line, produce a much more 'natural' look.

- You should know the reasons for clipping and how often you would need to clip a horse to keep it looking really tidy. (Element 8.2.1) Clipping becomes essential in the winter months when a horse grows a heavy winter coat and subsequently sweats if you work him. There are other reasons for clipping, associated with turnout for shows and reducing irritation to the skin for some skin conditions. Primarily clipping makes the cleaning and grooming of the competitive horse easier and improves his comfort.

- You should be familiar with the range of clips that are given to horses, according to the work they are doing and the conditions under which they are kept. (Element 8.3.1) You may be asked to identify a particular clip on a horse that is brought out in front of you, or to indicate on a horse where the hair would be removed and where it would remain. If asked to describe a blanket clip, for example, then you would suggest that this is ideal for a horse that is working

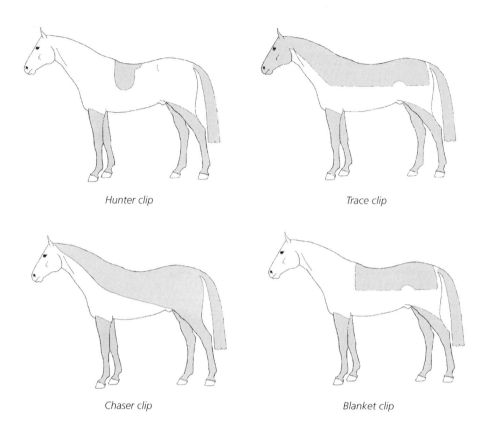

Hunter clip

Trace clip

Chaser clip

Blanket clip

quite hard but may also have to stand around at a competition and therefore needs some warmth over his back.

- You will probably be asked to handle a set of clippers and discuss how they are put together (how to fit and adjust blades and check the appliance for safety). (Elements 8.4.1 and 8.4.2) The safety of the machinery is of paramount importance and regular annual maintenance is advisable. You should have some ideas about how the clipping blades are maintained and where you could get this done.

- You may be asked about safety when clipping (Element 8.5.1), including what clothing might be appropriate and where would be a safe area in which to clip. You should be able to demonstrate your position in the stable with relation to the horse while clipping him. You may be asked about what assistance you might need when clipping the horse's head or under his belly, and what practical means of restraining him would be appropriate if he objected to being clipped.

How to become competent

- You may not have the opportunity to actually clip a horse but you **must** assist someone and ask them to allow you to use the clippers on a large part of the horse (flank or neck) so that you have actually handled the machinery.

- If you are in a full-time training situation, particularly in a commercial yard, you will almost certainly have the opportunity to practise the skills of clipping and trimming, which must be demonstrated to you in a 'hands-on' situation.

- Take the time to watch someone pulling a mane and tail. There is a skill and technique involved, which comes from watching someone competent and then practising yourself.

- If you have a chance to go into a yard where horses are prepared for showing classes then you will see manes and tails pulled and heels trimmed to a very high standard.

- Competence in clipping comes with practice. Make sure that you have handled the clipping machine as much as possible. Each brand of clippers is slightly different, but they are all largely similar. Practise removing the blades and replacing them. Take particular care not to lose any of the tiny parts. Always handle the blades either close to the floor (in a squatting position) or over a table, so that if you do drop any of the pieces they do not bounce off into oblivion and you lose them. Cutting blades can shatter easily if dropped.

- When you first start clipping, draw an outline of the clip on the horse using chalk or saddle soap. This allows you to follow the line easily, rather than having to clip it 'free hand' (which is unwise if you are not experienced). Use a numnah to outline the saddle patch if you are clipping the horse for a hunter clip.

- Start the clipping procedure on an 'easy' part of the horse – the shoulder or the neck – before progressing to areas where he might be more fractious. In the early stages of learning to clip ask someone more competent than you to assist and give you moral support.

- Make sure you know why a particular type of clip is used. If in doubt, ask questions. Frequency of clipping depends on many factors, including the time of year, amount of coat growth, weather, conditions in which the horse is kept (in or out), and how tidy you need him to look.

Anatomy and Physiology

The signs of health and ill-health.

The equine skeletal frame, the position of the horse's main internal organs.

A basic understanding of the horse's digestive system and the structure and function of the horse's foot.

ELEMENT

C	**9.1.1**	Outline the general health and condition of the horse in front of you.
S	**9.2.1**	Outline the horse's digestive system and basic function of individual parts.
C	**9.3.1**	Identify the horse's main internal organs.
S	**9.4.1**	Describe why bulk is important to the horse's digestive system.
S	**9.5.1**	Give the function of bacteria found in the hind-gut.
C	**9.6.1**	Identify the parts of the skeleton on the horse in front of you.
S	**9.7.1**	Give the principles of horse health.
S	**9.8.1**	Give the horse's normal temperature, pulse and respiration rates.
S	**9.9.1**	Describe how breathing can be an indication of health or ill-health.
S	**9.9.2**	Describe how eating can be an indication of health or ill-health.
S	**9.9.3**	Describe how droppings can be an indication of health or ill-health.
C	**9.9.4**	Describe how posture can be an indication of health or ill-health.
C	**9.10.1**	Describe the external parts of the horse's foot.

| S | **9.10.2** Explain the function of the frog. |

| S | **9.10.3** Explain the importance of the white line. |

What the examiner is looking for

- You must be able to look at a horse and describe the basic signs of good health. (Element 9.1.1) Try to be systematic in your description and then you won't forget anything. For example, start at the head and describe bright eyes, clear eyes and nose – no discharge – shiny, flexible coat, no apparent discomfort in stance, normal behaviour, normal eating/drinking, droppings texture and frequency, urine colour and ease of passing. These would be the most obvious signs that you should be able to describe.

- Consider what you mean by 'health' and 'condition' and make sure that you are clear in your explanation to the examiner. There can sometimes be a difference in people's interpretation of the term 'condition'. Does 'condition' mean 'health'? Not really. 'Health' refers to the state of well-being of the horse. 'Condition' relates more to the horse's state of fitness at the time (e.g. could he complete a one-day event or only walk gently around the lanes?), or to the amount of weight he is carrying. Make quite sure that when you discuss condition with your examiner, he or she knows exactly what you are talking about because you explain it so clearly.

- Be able to describe the horse's digestive system (Element 9.2.1), which starts from the horse taking the food in through his lips, biting the grass (if necessary) with his incisor teeth, chewing with the molar or grinding teeth and using his tongue to push the food around in his mouth. Again, be very clear on the progression of food through the horse's gut. You may be required to pick up the discussion half way through the process, so it is important that you listen to the other candidates and can carry on from wherever the person before you is asked to stop. A clear, basic understanding of the way each part of the system functions is important as it will help you to speak with confidence when describing the parts.

- Make sure that you know where in the horse's body each major organ lies. (Element 9.3.1) You should be able to indicate on the horse's body where a particular organ is and approximately how much room it takes up. The major organs that you are likely to be asked about include the heart, lungs, stomach,

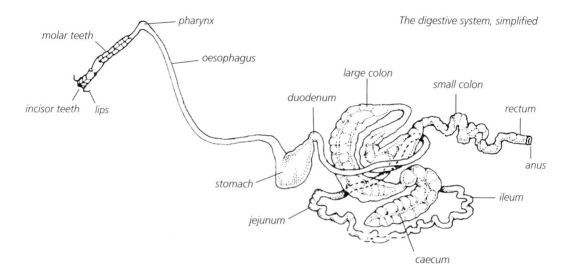

The digestive system, simplified

liver, kidneys and intestines. Is the stomach the size of a tennis ball or a rugby ball? (Make sure you know roughly what size a rugby ball is!)

- You may be asked about the importance of bulk to the function of the digestive system. (Element 9.4.1) Bulk enables the whole length of the digestive tract to keep moving. Without roughage there would be nothing to keep moving the other, softer or more easily rendered down materials through the system and it would slow down or stop.

- Know that the hind gut contains bacteria or 'gut flora' which assist in the digestion of the roughage in the diet. (Element 9.5.1) The health of the bacteria is partly dependent on the consistency of the horse's diet and the overall well-being of the horse.

- You must be familiar with the skeletal structure of the horse (Element 9.6.1), and you are likely to be asked about this in a stable, with a horse in front of you. You must know not only the names of the bones but also where the bones are in the body as you look at the horse. For example, the vertebrae in the neck do not sit along the crest of the neck, but come from the poll and are located well beneath the crest in the central part of the neck, with long spiny processes which extend back up to form the area we call the withers. Make sure that you have learned how many vertebrae there are, what the bones in the front and the hind legs are called, and learn them well. Guessing roughly where the bones are will not be good enough if you are asked to point them out exactly. Be able to pick up the

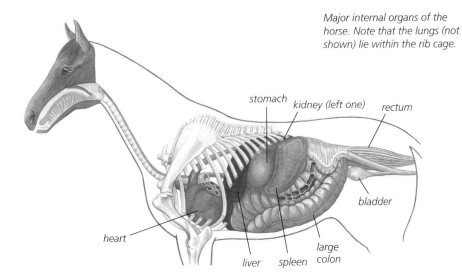

Major internal organs of the horse. Note that the lungs (not shown) lie within the rib cage.

stomach   kidney (left one)   rectum

bladder

heart

large colon

liver   spleen

discussion at any point – you may have to describe just the hind leg or a section of the back.

- The basic principles of horse health (Element 9.7.1) have already been considered in Element 9.1.1. Remember to include the horse's 'normal' behaviour traits – if any of his 'normalities' alter, it can indicate a change in health.

- Learn the horse's normal temperature, pulse and respiration rates and be able to relate these to his pattern of health. (Element 9.8.1) Normal readings would be in the following range:

    temperature – 38 °C (100.5 °F);

    pulse = heart rate – 38 to 42 beats per minute;

    respiration 8 to 12 breaths per minute (one complete inhalation and expiration = one breath)

- Know that an increase in the horse's normal breathing rate (at rest 8 to 12 breaths per minute) might indicate pain or distress, and, if linked to other symptoms, may indicate ill health. (Element 9.9.1)

- Be able to talk about how the horse's pattern of eating can reflect his good health or be a sign of change in his state of well-being. (Element 9.9.2) If a horse goes off his food for no apparent reason, with possible other developing symptoms, it may

The skeleton.

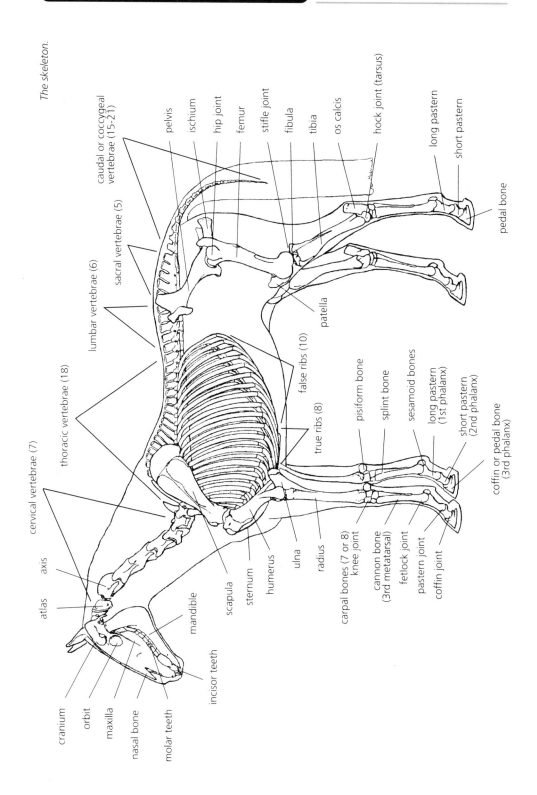

caudal or coccygeal vertebrae (15–21)

sacral vertebrae (5)

lumbar vertebrae (6)

thoracic vertebrae (18)

cervical vertebrae (7)

pelvis

ischium

hip joint

femur

stifle joint

fibula

tibia

os calcis

hock joint (tarsus)

long pastern

short pastern

pedal bone

patella

false ribs (10)

true ribs (8)

pisiform bone

splint bone

sesamoid bones

long pastern (1st phalanx)

short pastern (2nd phalanx)

coffin or pedal bone (3rd phalanx)

carpal bones (7 or 8) knee joint

cannon bone (3rd metatarsal)

fetlock joint

pastern joint

coffin joint

radius

ulna

humerus

sternum

scapula

atlas

axis

mandible

incisor teeth

cranium

orbit

maxilla

nasal bone

molar teeth

indicate a change in his state of good health.

- The state of the horse's droppings can show whether his digestive system is functioning well or whether there is an underlying problem or a developing problem. Know the appearance of 'normal' droppings and understand the changes in consistency and possible 'smell' that might indicate an impending change of health. (Element 9.9.3)

- Be able to recognise and discuss how a horse might stand if he is not healthy. Be aware that either constant moving around, apparently trying to find a comfortable stance, or an appearance that the horse is distributing weight awkwardly to 'save' one or more limbs, indicates a possible problem. (Element 9.9.4)

- Your knowledge of the skeleton must include the external parts of the foot. (Element 9.10.1) Be quite familiar and very practised at being able to describe each part of the foot and its basic function. (Element 9.10.2) This would include knowledge about the frog, whose essential function is to act as a 'pump', helping in recirculating blood back out of the foot, and also as a shock-absorber for the foot.

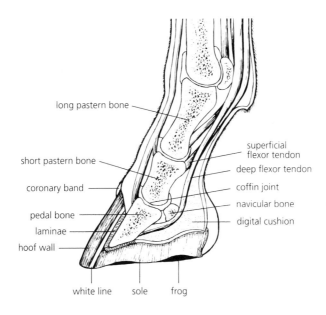

The foot and pastern. The bones of the lower leg, below the knee/hock, are identical in the front and hind limbs.

The sole of the foot.

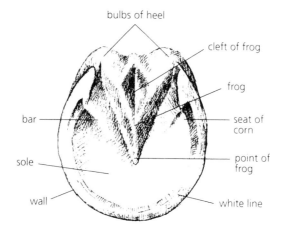

bulbs of heel

cleft of frog

frog

bar

seat of corn

sole

point of frog

wall

white line

- Be aware of the existence of the 'white line' (Element 9.10.3) and that, in simple terms, it defines the 'line' between the sensitive parts of the foot (the internal structures) and the external or insensitive parts. Be sure that you can find it on the foot (easier to do on an unshod foot), and understand its importance in relation to where the farrier's nails are driven to hold a shoe in place. Nails to keep a shoe on are driven into the insensitive part of the hoof.

How to become competent

- This is a section where you **must** take the time and the trouble to learn the physiological terms for the various bones in the body and the parts and functions of the digestive system.

- Then spend time looking at a horse and indicating where on the body the respective parts of the skeleton and the various organs lie.

- This section of the syllabus is one area where you can work with another person who is studying for Stage 2, helping and testing each other.

- From time to time reinforce your learning with your instructor, asking him/her to take you through the parts of the skeleton, the major organs and the digestive system, identifying correct locations and names.

- Practice picking up the skeleton or digestive system 'half way through'. Be able to describe just the bones of the hind leg. Be able to carry on the discussion on the digestive system from the start of the small intestine or from the hind gut to the end.

- Look at the difficult names like 'oesophagus', 'duodenum' and 'ileum', familiarise yourself with their spelling and pronunciation; similarly with the 'cervical vertebrae', 'sesamoid bones' and 'scapula'. As soon as you struggle or seem uncomfortable over any of these terms, you indicate a lack of confidence and an unfamiliarity in using these words – and that shows your lack of preparation. If you find yourself next to someone who has prepared this area very thoroughly, you may feel inadequate and this will cause you to fumble and falter even more.

Horse Behaviour

The value of calmness and kindness in establishing the horse's confidence and improving his well-being and therefore his work.

ELEMENT

10.1.1 Give examples of possible causes of unsettled behaviour in horses at grass during summer months.

10.2.1 Give examples of how by stabling the horse, we go against his natural lifestyle.

10.3.1 Describe the indications of nervousness in the horse in a variety of situations.

10.4.1 Describe safe methods of handling horses in a variety of situations.

10.5.1 Give examples of good yard practice when accommodating a new horse.

10.6.1 Describe why a normally stable-kept horse may be difficult to catch when he is out in a field.

10.7.1 Give reasons for anti-social behaviour in the horse when he is ridden in company.

10.8.1 Describe how the horse might behave if the tack doesn't fit.

What the examiner is looking for

- You should know that a horse living at grass in the summer months is likely to be disturbed by flies and biting insects, he may not like the heat and so be unsettled. (Element 10.1.1) If the ground becomes hard and the grass sparse then the unshod horse may show signs of being foot sore, and may become fractious because he has nothing to eat to occupy him.

- Be able to describe the horse's natural lifestyle, that he is basically a grazing, browsing, herd animal (Element 10.2.1) who enjoys living in a group and establishing his pecking order within the group. Stabling the horse actually disturbs that natural lifestyle. He may therefore demonstrate anxiety because he has no other horses around him. If you feed him only at specific times then he may develop repetitive habits to alleviate his boredom and fulfil his desire to 'eat' fairly regularly.

- You must be able to describe signs that indicate nervousness in the horse in a stabled situation, at grass, and out and about while being ridden. (Element 10.3.1) At grass, the horse can demonstrate his instinctive reaction, which is to run away from something he fears. In the stable he cannot run so he turns his bottom towards the perceived danger and 'threatens' with his back legs. When ridden, the horse may choose the option to 'buck' to try to dislodge something on his back of which he is afraid.

- Be aware that horses can be dangerous if not handled with knowledge, care and authority. (Element 10.4.1) It is wise to handle horses (particularly those you do not know or which are young or untrained) wearing gloves, and, in certain circumstances while leading them, also a riding hat (with harness fastened). Safe footwear when working around or handling horses is essential. Be able to discuss when to put a bridle on the horse instead of a headcollar, and when to use a lunge

Horses interacting. The horse on the left is being 'groomed' by the horse with the blaze. The recipient's contentment is indicated by the ears being forward and the submissive, lowered neck.

rein instead of a lead rope. Know some other methods by which you might assert greater authority and therefore control of the horse (e.g. lunge cavesson or Chifney).

- Know how you would integrate a new horse into your yard if he had never been there before. (Element 10.5.1) Recognise such things as putting the horse next door to a calm and settled horse will help the newcomer to settle. Provide food to occupy him and perhaps leave bandages or protective boots on the horse until he is familiar with his new home.

- You may be asked to discuss the behaviour you might see in a horse that is usually stabled when he is turned out in the field and is then difficult to catch. (Element 10.6.1) Such behaviour may stem from anxiety if the horse is not used to being free in the field, but it is more likely to be associated with the horse's desire to stay free in an environment which he prefers.

- Be able to discuss and recognise anti-social behaviour in the horse when being ridden. (Element 10.7.1) Traits you might be expected to discuss may include the horse being bad-tempered, laying his ears back at other horses close to him, and threatening them with his heels and/or teeth if they come too close behind him or beside him. These traits of 'bad' behaviour are usually associated with the inhibition of the horse's normal ability to assert himself in a 'pecking order' while being ridden. He may feel threatened by another horse invading 'his space' and coming close behind or beside him.

- You may be asked to describe how a horse might behave if his tack does not fit. (Element 10.8.1) Very simply, the horse is likely to be uncomfortable and even in pain, and any behaviour traits showing resistance will reflect this (e.g. refusing to go forward, appearing stiff in the back or unlevel in his steps, or showing resistance in his mouth).

How to become competent

- This is a 'hands on', practical section requiring awareness. You will achieve competence by observing and handling lots of horses in different situations.

- Never miss an opportunity to 'learn' about the horses you deal with. Never take them for granted and think you know them so well that you don't need to handle them with care and good practice. Horses react unpredictably to different conditions: weather, noise and unexpected activity can all affect the 'normal' behaviour of a horse. If you fail to regard these factors then sooner or later a horse will accidentally hurt you.

- Watch more experienced people manage young horses, stallions and perhaps spoilt horses that have come into your establishment for reschooling. Sometimes horses need to be reminded 'who is the boss'; they may need a short, sharp lesson in good manners. Horses learn through repetition and if they have been allowed to be unruly and rude, then they will continue to behave in this manner.

- Watch the way horses react and interact in the field and stable. Learn to 'read' the horse and be able to understand the way he is thinking – this will be the key to your competence as a horsemaster. You will then learn when to be firm and when to be sympathetic; you will know when the horse is being a 'brat' and when he is genuinely frightened and needs your reassurance. His confidence will then build from your competence.

- Always follow safe practical procedures. Don't take risks, and don't take horses for granted, assuming that they will always behave in a predictable way.

Horse Health

When a horse is off colour or is not sound enough to be worked.

Know the treatment of minor wounds and basic nursing and when to call the veterinary surgeon. Know the importance of regular worming.

ELEMENT

S   **11.1.1** Describe the symptoms of unsoundness in the horse.

C   **11.2.1** Describe the treatments for a variety of minor wounds.

C   **11.3.1** Give the rules of basic sick nursing.

C   **11.4.1** Give the indications that would necessitate a visit from the vet.

S   **11.5.1** Give a list of essential basic equine health records.

S   **11.6.1** Describe the indications of worm infestation in the horse.

C   **11.6.2** Give an appropriate worm control programme for the horse.

S   **11.7.1** Give the signs of a horse having problems with its teeth.

What the examiner is looking for

- You must be able to describe the signs or symptoms of a horse that is unsound or lame. (Element 11.1.1) The most obvious observation would be an irregular or unlevel gait (particularly visible in trot). Visible injury, heat or swelling in a limb, or heat in the foot and pain on pressure are also clear signs of a problem. Observation from in front of the horse and from behind is important to confirm your opinion. The horse may be more unsound on hard ground and less lame on soft ground, or vice versa. The irregularity may show intermittently or when the horse is asked to turn.

- Basic wound treatment must be studied (Element 11.2.1), and it is advisable to be able to describe the most up-to-date methods. Basic criteria for wound treatment would include assessing the damage, cleansing the wound and stopping bleeding as appropriate, calling the vet if stitching or anti-tetanus cover is needed, and keeping the wound clean and able to heal from the outside inwards.

- You may be asked to discuss how you would care for a horse that is ill or perhaps confined to his box due to injury. (Element 11.3.1) Good attention to detail would be essential to enable you to closely monitor the 'patient'. Good sick nursing would include having one person only to care for the horse and therefore be able to keep an ongoing check on the horse; fresh, deep bedding; fresh, clean water and feed; treatment according to the horse's condition, and veterinary advice if appropriate.

- You must have clear opinions about when you might need to call the vet (Element 11.4.1) as these could affect the well-being of a horse in your care. The main criteria which would guide your decision would be:

  - an acute rise in temperature with accompanying signs of illness or distress;

  - colic;

  - a wound of a severity which demanded professional care, e.g. profuse bleeding;

  - an acute injury or lameness which was causing the horse severe pain;

  - any condition which after a period of your management was not improving;

  - any condition that you are in doubt about.

- You should be able to discuss records that would essentially be maintained in any well-run yard. (Element 11.5.1) These would include some kind of system by which each horse in the yard had his own health records. These would cover when he was inoculated, when he was wormed, when he had his teeth attended to, and any other veterinary treatment that he received, either by your vet or a member of staff in the yard,.

- You should be aware that horses suffer from parasitic worm infestations, and that some kind of worming programme is important. (Element 11.6.1) A horse with a

Horse looking 'off colour' – dejected appearance, head low and expression dull; the rib cage looks 'tucked up' – drawn and uncomfortable.

Alert, healthy horse – bright expression, ears forward, body looking 'round' and at ease.

worm infestation may lose condition, have a stary coat and a 'pot' belly, and be not thriving generally. The potential for horses suffering from an infestation of worms is often reflected in poor pasture management as well. (See Element 14.2.1)

■ Be sure that you can discuss several acceptable worming programmes for horses (Element 11.6.2.) because today there is more than one opinion on effective worm management.

- Good management of the horse would include a regular check of the condition of his teeth. Problems with teeth may be suspected in a horse showing discomfort in the mouth, either when being bridled or while being ridden. He may eat slowly, or obviously not chew properly, with food slipping out of the sides of his mouth (quidding). He may be fractious and unsteady in his head, which is out of character with normal behaviour. (Element 11.7.1)

How to become competent

- If you are looking after one or more horses on a full-time basis, you will become very familiar with what is 'normal' for each horse in terms of health, well-being and behaviour. From this it is easy to recognise small signs of discomfort.

- Awareness of small changes and signs are the hallmark of a good horsemaster. Try to be observant to small indications, which might indicate the beginnings of a problem.

- Look at every horse that comes into the yard, whether at livery or to school, and consider its condition. Spend time watching horses moving (in the school under saddle, or when they are being led, even if this is only in or out of the field). You will then learn to recognise when a horse is irregular in its gaits.

- When you have the opportunity of handling or grooming any horse, get into the habit of running your hands down each of its four legs and feel how cool and un-puffy they are. If there are any slight lumps, bumps or swellings, ask your instructor to explain why they are there and whether they have a special name or not (e.g. windgalls). Get used to comparing legs (front and back) to see whether any 'heat' you may feel in one leg is isolated or is the same in the opposite leg.

- Similarly with the feet, feel the wall of the hoof and compare both front feet and then both back feet.

- Feeling heat and pain in a limb takes practice, as does improving your 'eye' for how the horse looks.

- Try to be involved in dealing with any minor wound treatments in the yard. In the event of a more serious incident, try to observe the management of the wound by senior members of staff and watch the vet work if he is called.

- Make sure that you have seen the yard records for each horse. Discuss with your instructor or the yard manager how the records are maintained and ask what sort of information is recorded and why.

- Make sure that you know what worming programme is used in your yard. Watch the worm doses being given and look at the products being used; ask your instructor why a certain product is used at that time of the year.

- Consider also what other measures are in place in your establishment to manage the pasture, which in turn assists in the control of worms.

- Find out how often the horses in your yard have their teeth checked and who treats them, if this is necessary.

- When it comes to studying horse health, try to gain hands-on experience as well, as this will make it much more 'real' and applicable. Ask questions about every aspect of horse health relevant to the above requirements and make sure that you look at as many horses as possible, especially if you have the chance to see some horses whose worm management may have been neglected.

Fittening

How to relate condition, feeding and progressive exercise when bringing a horse up from resting at grass into regular work.

The process of cooling off after work and roughing off a fit horse.

(Regular work: six hours per week at walk, trot and canter without stressing – refer to Examinations Handbook)

ELEMENT

C **12.1.1** Give an appropriate fittening programme for use when bringing a horse up from grass and into regular work.

C **12.2.1** Give the possible causes of coughs and colds when first bringing a horse up from grass.

C **12.2.2** Give the possible causes of saddle and girth galls when first bringing a horse up from grass.

C **12.2.3** Give the potential consequences of dust and/or diet change when first bringing a horse up from grass.

C **12.3.1** Give examples of feeding in relation to the fittening programme and condition of the horse, when bringing up from grass and into regular work.

C **12.4.1** Give a suitable programme for roughing off a fit horse.

S **12.5.1** Show awareness of the possible causes of concussion injuries when riding out.

S **12.5.2** Show awareness of the possible causes of strain injuries when riding out.

S **12.6.1** Give the procedure for cooling off the horse after work.

12.6.2 Outline care of the horse after work.

What the examiner is looking for

- By the time you are competent at Stage 2 level, you should be familiar with seeing, and hopefully being involved with, the fittening work of horses in your care. You must be able to clearly describe the gradual process by which a horse in 'soft' condition (i.e. one that has not been in regular work for some time) is developed in both exercise and feeding to become a horse that is capable of regular work. (Element 12.1.1)

- You will be expected to describe the value of an increasing period of walking exercise, then the introduction of trot, and from this the gradual development of canter to further the fitness process.

- You should understand the influences that affect the time it would take to develop fitness. These would include how long the horse has been out of work, what sort of type or breeding he is, how fat he is when you start, what facilities you have to develop the fitness work.

- You must be aware that horses brought into a stable having lived at grass, may be susceptible to coughs or colds due to the change in environment. (Elements 12.2.1 and 12.2.3) You should have ideas as to how this risk can be minimised. These would include gradually bringing the horse in for increasingly longer periods in the stable, keeping the stable well ventilated and feeding damp hay and feed, to minimise the risk of dust inhalation causing irritation and coughing. Be aware of the horse's digestive system (check droppings) to make sure that the change in diet is not having a negative effect.

- You will be expected to discuss the potential risk of the horse developing sores, or 'galls', where skin contact is made with tack when the horse is unused to wearing equipment. (Element 12.2.2) Know the precautions you would take to minimise this, such as careful management of the tack to keep it supple and comfortable, the use of soft numnahs and girths, and taking great care with the fitting of tack to fat, unfit horses.

- You will be asked about the gradual development of the horse's feed ration in relation to the increase of work, bearing in mind that the field-kept horse's diet is likely to have been exclusively grass. You must be able to describe how you would gradually introduce hard food, and some kind of bulk ration such as hay or haylage as the horse becomes stabled for longer periods. (Element 12.3.1)

- You should have some knowledge of feeds which would be appropriate to the gradual development of a fitter horse. You may be asked to recognise feed samples (see Element 15).

- The reverse process of fittening is 'roughing off'. You are likely to be asked about this procedure, and you should recognise that the roughing-off programme can be achieved in a considerably shorter period of time than the building up of fitness. (Element 12.4.1) Be able to discuss the effects of weather, time of year, type of horse and facilities available in the planning of a roughing-off programme.

- You may be asked about the possible risk of injury when getting a horse fitter. Roadwork carries risks of subjecting the horse to concussion, which may result in an injury such as a splint. (Element 12.5.1) Working a horse in heavy ground or uneven going, before his limbs are fit enough to cope, can leave him at risk of strain injuries to muscles, tendons or ligaments. (Element 1.2.5.2)

- The gradual cooling off of the horse after a period of work, especially when he has exerted himself to the point of sweating, is important, as is the general care of the horse after work. (Elements 12.6.1 and 12.6.2) Make sure you can discuss clearly

Roadwork is often an important part of developing a horse's fitness. Exercising in pairs keeps horses content and confident.

a system for bringing the horse back to his stable, having walked him to the point of him being cool, dried off and not blowing. This would include loosening the girth and throwing a light rug or anti-sweat sheet over him to prevent him becoming chilled.

How to become competent

- It is important not only that you read up about how to develop fitness in the horse, but also that you experience it by actually doing it.

- Be able to recognise the horse that is in 'soft' condition – what he looks like, what he 'feels' like – both when you groom him and apply his tack.

- Learn to recognise what the horse 'feels' like when you first ride him after a period of being out of work. This 'feel' should then follow through as the horse begins to develop fitness. He will find his work easier, he will sweat less, he will start to lose his flab and fat and become more muscled and streamlined in his physique.

- Recognise the difference in the horse in the stable – he will look different as he loses weight and becomes more toned in his muscles. He may change a little in character as he feels more 'full of himself' – he may nip when his girth is tightened, as his rugs are applied or when he is groomed.

- Look at different horses in your yard and find out what work they are doing; then look at their build and physique, feel their condition in terms of their coat and muscular tone and firmness. The legs of a horse that is developing fitness and of a fit horse in regular work, should be cool, firm and not showing any heat or puffiness.

- In the unfortunate event that a horse does develop any type of injury due to the fittening process, make sure that you look at the injury and then discuss the cause and subsequent treatment and management with your instructor or stable manager.

General Knowledge

The Country Code, safety measures and correct procedures when riding on the public highway. The correct procedures in the event of an accident.

Know the aims and structure of The British Horse Society and the benefits of membership.

ELEMENT

C	**13.1.1** Describe safe procedures when riding on the highway.
C	**13.1.2** Describe your procedure when riding onto or turning off a major road.
C	**13.1.3** List high-visibility equipment suitable for use when riding on the roads.
C	**13.2.1** Give examples of good behaviour when riding on bridleways.
S	**13.2.2** Give examples of correct action when meeting others on tracks and bridleways.
S	**13.3.3** List the aims of The British Horse Society.
S	**13.3.2** List the departments in The British Horse Society.
C	**13.4.1** Describe the action to be taken in the event of an accident on your yard.

What the examiner is looking for

- As mentioned at the start of this book, a pre-requisite of taking the Stage 2 exam is that you hold the Riding and Road Safety certificate. Achievement in this test ensures that you have studied, trained and shown your ability in theoretical knowledge in a simulated test, and then on the public highway on a horse. With this under your belt, any questions you get on this subject in your Stage 2 exam should not give you any cause for concern.

■ Make sure that you can describe safe riding procedures on the road. (Element 13.1.1) Read the latest edition of *Riding and Roadcraft* to familiarise yourself with all the points of safety. These include:

- good preparation of yourself, and of your horse in terms of tack, clothing and the condition of the horse's feet;

- good manners on the road with regard to acknowledging and thanking other road users, particularly those who are courteous and helpful;

- safe positioning of you and your horse at all times;

- clear signals given in good time to ensure understanding of your intentions by other road users;

- good judgement of what to do when, to maintain safety for yourself and others on the road.

■ You may be asked to describe or perhaps even demonstrate your procedure for making a turn. (Element 13.1.2) Remember: observation all around you is the first thing you need to do – and this observation should be ongoing throughout your road riding. After observation, a clear hand signal would be necessary, followed by your control through the turn, maintaining a watchful eye for any possible change of conditions as you execute the turn with both hands back on the reins.

■ Discuss the equipment that you think is helpful and suitable for riding on the road. (Element 13.1.3) Any high visibility clothing is valuable; avoid wearing dark clothing, especially on dull days. Specially designed fluorescent clothing is essential. Tabards, hat covers and jackets are all available for the rider. Exercise rugs, boots, reins and stirrup lights can all be used on the horse for increased visibility.

■ You should know that good behaviour when riding out and about is always to be recommended for the benefit of all users of roads or bridleways. (Element 13.2.1) Always close gates securely. Ride along designated paths or along the headland of a field if there are crops sown. Ride around stock at the walk, never in a way that will disturb cattle or sheep. Keep the pace slow if there are other riders nearby or

Riding on the road. Safety can be greatly improved by using specialised fluorescent high-visibility clothing on yourself and your horse.

if a fast pace is likely to cut up the ground.

- When meeting others on tracks and bridleways (Element 13.2.2) always make sure they know you are there (if approaching from behind). Slow down and request permission to pass them, and go on away from them. Take care when passing other horses, especially those unknown to you.

- The aims of The British Horse Society (Element 13.3.1) can be listed as:

  - to improve the general standard of horse/pony welfare in Great Britain;

  - to improve awareness of horses in general;

  - to improve standards of riding and horse knowledge through training and education;

  - to improve safety for all riders;

  - to improve access for all riders and carriage drivers;

  - to provide benefits for members of the Society.

- You must be able to describe the procedure that would be carried out in the event of an accident in your yard. This should include

  - assessing the situation as quickly as possible;

- going to the injured person;

- deciding whether any additional help is needed (in which case summon it, including paramedic help, if necessary);

- reassuring the injured party and administering first aid as appropriate;

- after dealing with the incident, making a full and comprehensive report of the incident, both in writing and verbally, to any senior member of staff, with support from witnesses as required.

How to become competent

- This is another 'practical' area that will be much easier to talk about if you have 'done it' and can speak from experience. The Riding and Road Safety training will be invaluable, but it is important that you go out and gain experience of riding out on roads and bridleways. It is always nicer to ride out with one or more friends, and this also enables you to look after each other.

- Depending on the area in which you live, there will be regional variations in the type of riding country you have available and also the amount of traffic you have to encounter.

- Try to make sure that any horses you ride on the road are reliable in traffic. If you are introducing a young horse to roadwork for the first time, or you have a horse that is nervous in traffic, make sure that you take a highly reliable horse (and rider) out with you to act as a 'nanny'.

- If you can access good off-road riding then this is ideal, as any road riding can be hazardous.

- Make sure that you are clear as to the structure of The British Horse Society. Be aware that as well as the Training and Examinations department which organises and administrates exams like Stage 2, the BHS also has Safety, Welfare, Access, Riding Schools, Recreational Riding and Membership departments. It manages the British Riding Clubs organisation with affiliation of numerous riding clubs throughout the whole of the UK. The benefits of BHS membership are that you are contributing to the biggest membership organisation for the well-being of the horse in the UK and as a member you receive a good rate of insurance cover for personal liability and personal accident. There are legal and tax helplines, and a range of advice is available in published leaflets on subjects of importance for the welfare and management of horses. Regional Development Officers and a structure of county committees offer local activities and advice if needed.

- Make sure that you are fully briefed on the accident procedure in place at your establishment. You should know where the accident book is kept and should have been briefed on how to complete it. In the event of an accident make sure that a more senior member of staff has overseen or helped you fill in the full details of the incident as it occurred. Most incidents/accidents will usually be minor and of no lasting consequence; however, the recording of all incidents is essential.

Grassland Care

Have basic knowledge of good pasture and its maintenance. Know plants which are poisonous to horses.

ELEMENT

C **14.1.1** Describe the ideal field that would be suitable for horses.

S **14.2.1** Give examples of good practice when maintaining good quality grazing.

C **14.3.1** Describe common poisonous plants that may be found in and around grazing land.

What the examiner is looking for

- You must be able to describe what you consider to be the 'ideal' field for a horse(s) to live in. The main points of discussion you should be able to elaborate a little on would be: size of field relative to the number of horses, condition of grass, availability of water supply and shelter, gate access, and type of fencing. (Element 14.1.1)

- Having described what you consider to be good quality grazing (e.g. even growth of sward, variety of quality grasses, absence of weeds) you must then know that regular maintenance is essential to sustain and promote the quality of the grass. This would include: regular rotation of stock to allow rest and recuperation of the grass, regular removal of droppings, seasonal harrowing, rolling and if necessary treatment with seed, lime or fertiliser appropriate to advice given on the subject. (Element 14.2.1)

- You should be able to recognise and describe the most common poisonous plants indigenous to British horse pastures or surrounding environments. These would include: Ragwort, Foxglove, Deadly Nightshade, Hemlock, Buttercup, Yew, Laburnum, Bracken and Acorns. (Element 14.3.1)

How to become competent

- If taking Stage 2, you should be involved in some regular care of horses/ponies living and working from grass as well as caring for stabled horses. Make sure that you take responsibility for regularly checking the field in which these animals live for the maintenance of the basic facilities on which they rely.

POISONOUS PLANTS

Bracken

Yew

Laburnum

Ragwort

Foxglove

Deadly
Nightshade

- Be aware of the condition and maintenance of the fencing (particularly in winter when leaves off trees and hedges may allow weak areas and gaps to appear). Notice how in winter, when gateways become muddy and areas where horses are fed on the ground become poached, the quality of what the horses have to eat is reduced and the grazing limited. These areas may need some reseeding in the spring.

- Be aware that in the spring, as the ground dries and the sun promotes new growth, poisonous plants may develop; vigilant checking of the fields on a regular basis is needed.

- Get into the habit of observing horse paddocks and fields. Assess their good and bad points. Consider what features you would keep and what you would have to change if you chose to rent that field.

- Be aware of the variation in types of grassland according to the area in which you live. In a lowland area, where drainage may be less efficient, you may see many more reed-like grasses, which may not be of such good quality compared to a well-drained field in a fertile part of the country. Similarly, a field in a moorland or mountainous part of the country (parts of Wales or Scotland) may have sparse soil with poor grass.

- Consider fencing that is 'ideal' in terms of security and safety for the horses (e.g. post and rail) against what might be more affordable and provide greater protection from weather (an existing thick hedge).

- Similarly, be able to weigh up the pros and cons of different water supplies, and take into account what might be available (e.g. water trough or an existing stream).

Barbed-wire fence and damaged gate would offer potential danger to horses in the field.

Post and rail fence and a well-hung, secure gate would offer a safe environment for horses in this field.

- Be observant and practise running through the points in your mind as if you had been asked to give an opinion on the strengths and weaknesses of what you see. This is what you will need to be able to do with the examiner, so you must know your subjects thoroughly.

Watering and Feeding

Know:

The advantages and disadvantages of various watering systems and the importance of water to the horse.

Know a variety of common feedstuffs and their respective values.

Have a practical knowledge of how to prepare specific feedstuffs.

Know the basic principles of feeding old or sick horses, and horses and ponies at grass in all seasons.

Know how to make a simple feed chart.

ELEMENT

C	**15.1.1**	Give the rules of watering.
S	**15.1.2.**	Give examples of a variety of watering systems and their advantages/disadvantages.
C	**15.2.1**	Give the rules of feeding and describe their importance.
S	**15.3.1**	Assess the quality of a variety of feed samples.
S	**15.4.1**	Give examples of feedstuffs that have a heating effect.
S	**15.4.2**	Give examples of feedstuffs that have a fattening effect.
S	**15.4.3**	Give examples of feedstuffs that are suitable for horses doing fast work.
C	**15.5.1**	Give a suitable supplementary diet for a horse/pony living at grass during the winter.
S	**15.6.1.**	Give examples of suitable feed for old horses.
S	**15.6.2**	Give examples of suitable feed for sick horses.
C	**15.7.1**	Describe how to prepare sugar beet for feeding.

S   **15.7.2** Describe how to prepare a bran mash.

S   **15.7.3** Give the reasons for feeding soaked hay.

S   **15.7.4** Describe how to prepare soaked hay.

C   **15.8.1** Name and describe an alternative to hay in the horse's diet.

C   **15.9.1** Describe how to make a feed chart.

What the examiner is looking for

- Knowledge of feeding and watering the horse is one of the most basic and essential areas of horsemastership. It is therefore important that you are able to describe clearly and with good understanding, the knowledge underpinning this subject.

- In the wild, the horse will access water at will. Stabled (and, to a degree, at grass) the horse needs you to provide for him. (Element 15.1.1) A clean, fresh source is the first priority, then clean utensils and regular renewal (for the stabled horse). You should be aware of the horse's intake on a daily basis so that you can recognise any changes that might indicate a problem in health. Care when offering water to a hot or tired horse is important. Horses should have constant access to water but it is preferable that they do not imbibe a large amount immediately after eating their concentrate ration.

- You should know that water can be offered in buckets, larger plastic containers and a variety of automatic drinking systems. (Element 15.1.2) In fields, water might be provided in automatic self-filling drinking troughs, some type of refillable large container, or through a natural source such as a stream. Be able to discuss the pros and cons of all these methods and any others you have experienced. The siting of the water source in a field is also a point for discussion.

- You should be able to discuss the basic rules by which feeding of the horse is governed. (Element 15.2.1.) These include:

  • feed according to size, age, type and temperament;

  • feed according to work done;

  • feed little and often;

- make sure that water is provided or accessible before feeding;

- feed good quality fodder;

- feed at regular times;

- use clean feeding utensils;

- feed plenty of bulk in the ration;

- feed something succulent every day.

■ Consider each of these 'rules' and make sure that you can give a clear reason to support each one. Be able to pick up on any of these rules in any order, as this is how you are likely to be in the group theory section of your exam (see programme for the exam). Get into the habit of recalling each of the rules at random, then if seven or eight rules have already been given, you will be able to recall the elusive one or two that have not been mentioned.

■ You are likely to be offered feed samples to look at. Often these are contained in glass jars and the samples may have been there quite a long time! If this is the case, the smell and appearance of the feed may not be as fresh as you would choose for your horse. (Element 15.3.1) Be able to recognise the feed and give a brief description of when and for what sort of horse the food might be used. (Elements 15.4.1,15.4.2 and 15.4.3) Learn which feeds have a 'heating effect' on a horse (e.g. oats and maize). Learn which feeds have a fattening effect (e.g. barley). Know which feeds are considered suitable for horses doing fast work (e.g. oats and proprietary high energy competition mixes).

■ Feeding horses and ponies that live at grass and are required to work from grass needs some consideration, and the examiner will seek this knowledge. (Element 15.5.1) Be aware of the bulk requirement for these horses, particularly when the nutritional quality of the grass is low in winter. Good quality meadow hay or perhaps oat straw, with some concentrate feed, would be a consideration. Prepared mixes and cubes are often the best ration for horses/ponies at grass, although traditional straight feeds such as bruised barley, chaff and sugar beet also have a value.

■ Know about feeding old and sick horses, which again need specialist consideration. (Elements 15.6.1 and 15.6.2). Old horses need to be kept warm and maintain their body weight to assist this. They may also suffer from deterioration of their grinding teeth (molars) and so the bulk ration may need careful thought. Sick horses need to be tempted to eat to maintain strength and may need easily digested feeds or feeds which do not require much 'effort' to eat. Sick horses that are confined to their stables will also need careful management to ensure that their digestive system continues to function efficiently.

- You may be asked about the preparation of certain feeds. (Elements 15.7.1 and 15.7.2) Sugar beet is a valuable feed but needs care in preparation and management or it can ferment and cause problems. Know the difference between sugar-beet shreds and cubes and the length of time each needs to be soaked. Bran mashes were used extensively for many types of working horse until the huge development of knowledge in the horse's digestion of food and the nutritional content of feeds. Bran mashes are now used less frequently, but it is still important that you have a knowledge of the use of bran, know how to make a bran mash and understand where it has an application in the modern management of horses.

Preparing sugar beet.

dry sugar-beet shreds	*add ¾ bucket of water*	*leave overnight (10–12 hrs) and dry matter will swell, absorbing water to give this volume*

- You will be asked about the feeding of hay as a bulk ration (Elements 15.7.3,15.7.4 and 15.8.1), when and why it might need to be soaked, and how this would be done. Remember that hay should only be soaked for a short time to damp the spores that may cause an allergic reaction in the horse (20 to 30 mins would be the maximum time required). Hay can be 'soaked' by

    • immersing it – in a suitable container and then draining it;

    • spraying it – using a hosepipe over a filled haynet for some minutes;

    • steaming it – pouring boiling water into a sealed plastic sack containing the hay and allowing the steam to cool and permeate through the hay.

- An alternative to hay, which is extensively used in feeding horses, is haylage. (Element 15.8.1) This is also a conserved forage, but it has a higher water content than hay as a result of being cut from an earlier growth of grass and then being vacuum sealed in a plastic-wrapped bale.

- You should be able to discuss the simple structure of a feed chart. (Element 15.9.1) This would include the horse's name, how many times a day he is fed, the bulk ration and when this is given, the concentrate feeds and how many scoops or lbs/kg of food is allocated in each feed. Any additional items such as salt, succulents or vitamin/mineral additives would also be listed. The chart must provide enough information that someone who is not familiar with the horse could feed from the chart if need be.

How to become competent

- Feeding is an art, but as with any art you must learn the theory behind the practice. Learn the rules for feeding and watering so that they come automatically to mind. Familiarise yourself with as many different types of feed samples as you can.

- Study the feed chart in your yard; discuss which horses have what rations and why, with the stable manager or your instructor.

- Take an interest in the horses that you ride and what feed they are given. In due course you will then learn to adjust the feed ration according to how the horse looks (if he needs to put weight on or is too fat then the feed may need adjusting). You will realise that the way the horse 'feels' when you ride him may be affected by what feed he is eating.

- Become interested in the different prepared feeds that are on the market these days. Most feed companies provide extensive literature on all their products; collect this paperwork and read it. It can give you background information on the nutrients available in each feed and this will help you in due course when this information is required from you at Stage 3.

- Consider how horses are fed both at grass and in the stable. In winter, grass-kept horses need care with regard to noticing their condition and monitoring how much they are fed, particularly when the weather is freezing and if snow falls.

Stage 2
Riding

Syllabus

Candidates are required to demonstrate their ability to ride a quiet, experienced horse or pony in an enclosed space without assistance. Their balance and security should indicate the correct foundation for future progress.

Candidates who are considered to be well below the standard may be asked to retire.

IMPORTANT: Candidates are advised to check that they are working from the latest examination syllabus, as examination content and procedure are liable to alteration. Contact the BHS Examinations Office for up-to-date information regarding the syllabus.

BHS Stage 2 (Riding) – Syllabus

Candidates are required to demonstrate their ability to ride a quiet, experienced horse or pony in an enclosed space without assistance. Their balance and security should indicate the correct foundation for future progress. *Candidates who are considered to be below the standard may be asked to retire.*

Unit code number S2RIDI		
Learning Outcomes	**Element**	**Assessment criteria**
The candidate should be able to:		The candidate has achieved this outcome because s/he can:
	1.1.1	Demonstrate correct posture in the saddle
Ride a quiet experienced horse with an appropriate independent balance, depth and security of position	1.1.2	Show basic suppleness as required in the riding position
	1.2.1	Show an independent balance is maintained through turns, circles and transitions
Ride a quiet experienced horse forward at the correct speed for each gait	2.1.1	Show rhythm and balance are maintained through turns and circles
	2.2.1	Demonstrate ability to ride forward
	2.3.1	Know when and when not to use artificial aids (whip)
Ride a quiet experienced horse with an appropriate rein length both with and without stirrups, and with the reins in one hand.	3.1.1	Show non restricting yet controlling rein contact
	3.2.1	Show balance and security without stirrups in walk, trot and canter
	3.3.1	Show co-ordinated aids when riding with the reins in one hand
Ride a quiet experienced horse applying correct aids for canter leads and school figures	4.1.1	Show co-ordinated aid application
	4.1.2	Show preparation when making transitions
	4.2.1	Show correct canter strike-offs
	4.3.1	Show correctly sized school figures
Ride in harmony a quiet experienced horse.	5.1.1	Demonstrate calm, confident riding in establishing horse's trust
	5.2.1	Show fluent unconstrained work of the horse
Ride in the open and jump adopting safe procedures throughout.	6.1.1	Demonstrate ability to ride safely in company
	6.1.2	Demonstrate awareness of rules for riding in the open as well as in enclosed areas with others
	6.2.1	Demonstrate an appropriately balanced position when riding over undulating ground
	6.3.1	Show an ability to ride forward and influence gaits appropriately when riding in the open
	6.3.2	Demonstrate an awareness of undulating ground and weather conditions on a horse's balance
Jump a quiet experienced horse with an appropriate rein length and contact, correct length stirrup and ability to use the legs.	7.1.1	Demonstrate an appropriate length of stirrup for riding over undulating ground and around a course of fences
	7.2.1	Show effective use of leg aids when riding over undulating ground and around a course of fences
	7.3.1	Show correct application of rein aids when riding over undulating ground and around a course of fences
	7.3.2	Show correct use of the reins during all phases of the jump (approach, take-off, flight, landing and departure)
Jump a quiet experienced horse with security and balance, showing fold and follow over a fence.	8.1.1	Demonstrate correct forward jumping position when riding over undulating ground and around a course of fences
	8.1.2	Demonstrate a secure position when jumping
	9.1.1	Show effective control of pace
	9.2.1	Identify when and when not to use artificial aids (whip)
Jump in harmony a quiet experienced horse, whilst riding correct lines of approach towards and departures from fences.	10.1.1	Show effective calm confident riding while jumping
	10.2.1	Show a fluently ridden course
	10.3.1	Demonstrate awareness of the importance of correct canter leads

Influence column:
1.1.1 Compulsory; 1.1.2 Supporting; 1.2.1 Supporting; 2.1.1 Supporting; 2.2.1 Compulsory; 2.3.1 Supporting; 3.1.1 Supporting; 3.2.1 Compulsory; 3.3.1 Supporting; 4.1.1 Compulsory; 4.1.2 Supporting; 4.2.1 Compulsory; 4.3.1 Supporting; 5.1.1 Supporting; 5.2.1 Supporting; 6.1.1 Compulsory; 6.1.2 Supporting; 6.2.1 Compulsory; 6.3.1 Compulsory; 6.3.2 Supporting; 7.1.1 Supporting; 7.2.1 Compulsory; 7.3.1 Compulsory; 7.3.2 Supporting; 8.1.1 Compulsory; 8.1.2 Compulsory; 9.1.1 Compulsory; 9.2.1 Compulsory; 10.1.1 Supporting; 10.2.1 Compulsory; 10.3.1 Supporting

The candidate should be able to:

Ride a quiet experienced horse with an appropriate independent balance, depth and security of position.

ELEMENT

C	**1.1.1** Demonstrate correct posture in the saddle.
S	**1.1.2** Show basic suppleness as required in the riding position.
S	**1.2.1** Show an independent balance is maintained through turns, circles and transitions.

What the examiner is looking for

- A basically correct riding position is the foundation for all your work and your future as an effective, competent rider. (Element 1.1.1) You will be expected to show this as a Stage 2 level rider.

- The rider must sit centrally in the saddle with even weight on both seat bones, with level stirrups and even weight on the balls of the feet, the heel a little deeper

Correct basic riding position. Note straight line ear–shoulder–hip–heel; and also elbow–wrist–rein–horse's mouth.

than the toe. The upper body should rise tall and supple above the seat, with an imaginary vertical line from the rider's ear, through the shoulder, hip and heel. Hands should be level above the wither, with another imaginary straight line running from the elbow, through the wrist, the rein and to the horse's mouth. Hands should be closed around the reins, with the thumbs uppermost and the wrist relaxed.

- A good basic riding position shows some suppleness and relaxation. (Element 1.1.2) This is achieved through the secure development of the position. You must show an ability to follow the movement of the horses you ride, maintaining elasticity and 'feel' for the horse's movement under you.

- You must show an independent seat, which at no time, or in any of the basic gaits, is reliant on the reins. (Element 1.2.1) This independence must be demonstrated on at least two different horses on the flat and on two horses jumping. You will be asked to ride school movements to include turns, circles and transitions. These must demonstrate your independence and balance with the horse.

How to become competent

- The only way to develop a deeper, more secure riding position is to ride as much as possible. Try to ride under instruction on a regular basis so that your instructor can help you to improve and work on your position. It is easy, otherwise, to slip into bad habits, which can easily become established as firm faults and are then difficult to correct.

- If you can be lunged regularly, this is an ideal way of being able to work on your position and 'feel' without having to concentrate on the control of the horse.

- Ride as many different horses as you can to give you experience and confidence in being able to ride any horse that might be offered to you.

- Work regularly without your stirrups so that you progressively develop a deeper, more secure and more supple position.

- Ride horses out and about, hacking and in any type of off-road country, where you can truly develop your skill and control in the 'big outdoors'.

- Ride in a group fairly often. Be careful that you do not spend too long riding in a school with no other riders present. This does not develop your independence in terms of finding space and becoming competent when several other riders are using the same space.

- Practise school movements at every opportunity. Make sure that your preparation for turns, circles and transitions is good. The way in which you prepare and execute movements says much about your awareness, feel and effect as a rider.

The candidate should be able to:

Ride a quiet experienced horse forward at the correct speed for each gait.

ELEMENT

S **2.1.1** Show rhythm and balance are maintained through turns, circles and transitions.

C **2.2.2** Demonstrate ability to ride forward.

S **2.3.1** Know when and when not to use artificial aids (whip).

What the examiner is looking for

- Throughout all your riding you must try to establish a rapport and a partnership with each horse you ride. This is not easy when you may be nervous, and when you ride the horse for only a brief period of about 20 minutes. Prioritise riding the horse forward (Element 2.2.2) into an active gait and then concentrate on maintaining as good a rhythm (regularity) as you can. (Element 2.1.1)

- Be prepared to use your legs effectively, and if the horse is lazy and unresponsive to your legs, then demonstrate your ability to use your whip with good timing to remind the horse that he must obey your leg. (Element 2.3.1)

- Having established a forward-going and rhythmical gait then use this to

Riding a good-shaped circle, with the horse maintaining a consistent bend following the perimeter line of the circle.

demonstrate that you can ride well prepared and accurate turns and circles. When riding school figures you must show that you are aware of the tempo (speed of the pace) and can sustain the rhythm and balance of the horse within the movements. (Element 2.1.1)

How to become competent

- To be really confident in your riding ability at this level, you should be riding as often as possible. Ideally this should be every day, but realistically it may be four or five times per week.

- Riding under instruction will progress your technical competence, because the input from your instructor should consolidate your knowledge of what you are trying to achieve with the horse. Training will also ensure that you do not develop bad faults or habits in your riding position and in your overall manner of preparing and executing movements.

- It is very important that you ride as many horses as possible, and that, whenever you can, you ride under your own initiative. This will help you to develop independence and self sufficiency.

- It is easy to become dependent on your instructor and use him or her as a support to your riding competence. It is vital that you feel equally secure in your ability to produce good work whether you ride alone or under instruction. You will then feel confident in an exam situation when you may be nervous and you have no support from your instructor to keep you going.

- Ride in the school and hack out. Take part in whatever ridden activities you can, such as pleasure rides, clear-round jumping or riding club type competitions. Doing so will develop your all-round skills as a rider.

- If you have your own horse and are a regular competitor in any discipline then this will also prove extremely helpful. The more riding you have done independently, learning to 'feel' and find out about the horse from your own experience, the more this will consolidate and complement good training.

The candidate should be able to:

Ride a quiet, experienced horse with an appropriate rein length, both with and without stirrups, and with the reins in one hand.

ELEMENT

| S | **3.1.1** Show non-restricting yet controlling rein contact. |

| C | **3.2.1** Show balance and security without stirrups in walk, trot and canter. |

| S | **3.3.1** Show co-ordinated aids when riding with the reins in one hand. |

What the examiner is looking for

- Rein contact comes from your ability to ride the horse forward effectively in balance and rhythm and then to be secure and independent enough in your position to be able to maintain a good contact with the horse's mouth. (Element 3.1.1)

- The 'connection' with the horse's mouth **must** come from riding forward from leg to hand. (Element 2.2.1)

Reins rather long, so contact is slack; rider's hands almost in her waist.

Reins too short. Rider showing tension in the arms and restricting the horse, who is tight and short in the neck.

A good working length of rein – elbow and wrist in line with the horse's mouth, through an elastic connection in the rein.

- The reins must be short enough that you demonstrate a consistent connection, but the contact is always established from the activity of the horse's hind legs. You must be able to demonstrate an 'allowing hand', i.e. one which 'feels' the mouth but does not hang on to it or restrict the horse. (Element 3.1.1)

- You will be required to ride without your stirrups in walk, trot and canter. During this work you must show a depth and security of position that allows you to maintain an independent hand. (Element 3.2.1) Your position must be established enough to demonstrate a suppleness and ability to 'move' with the horse with no dependence on the reins to sustain balance.

- The independence of your seat will be further proved when you are asked to ride with the reins in one hand. (Element 3.3.1) Take the reins in your outside hand

and allow your inside hand to hang loosely down by your side. The relaxation in your fingers (of the free hand) shows your suppleness and co-ordination. When you change the rein, change the reins into the other hand also, so that the inside hand is free. You must be able to maintain balance and control of the horse while you have the reins in one hand.

How to become competent

- Ride as often as you can without stirrups. Ideally you should spend a little time on this every time you ride. You will then feel entirely comfortable without your stirrups. If you have regularly worked through all three paces on a variety of different horses, it should feel as familiar to you to ride without your stirrups as with them.

Reins in one hand, the free hand relaxed by the rider's side and the position well maintained. The free hand should not carry the whip.

- Similarly, practise riding with the reins in one hand. We all need to work on our co-ordination to some degree and the more often you practise a skill, the more competent you become.

- Practise riding figures and changes of direction with the reins in one hand. Feel familiar doing this on more than one horse. Make sure that you can also manage your whip when your reins are in one hand. (Either hold the whip under the thumb of your rein hand – but down the opposite side of the neck – or change the whip over to the outside hand as usual before putting the reins in one hand.) **Do not** carry the whip in your free hand.

The candidate should be able to:

Ride a quiet, experienced horse, applying correct aids for canter leads and school figures.

ELEMENT

C   **4.1.1** Show co-ordinated aid application.

S   **4.1.2** Show preparation when making transitions.

C   **4.2.1** Show correct canter strike-offs.

S   **4.3.1** Show correctly sized school figures.

What the examiner is looking for

- Correct and co-ordinated application of aids comes from a secure, independent position giving the ability to clearly apply leg and hand aids in a manner to which the horse can smoothly and obediently respond. (Element 4.1.1)

- You must have a clear understanding of what aids you are trying to apply for specific transitions or school movements, then show that you can apply them in a co-ordinated way.

- Co-ordinated aid application comes from good preparation. (Element 4.1.2) Preparation begins with the thought process: think in plenty of time **ahead** of when you require the movement or transition to happen. This will enable you to consider the aids you wish to apply, give you time to apply those aids in a smooth, clear way, and allow time for the horse to recognise the aids and respond to them. The end result should be smooth transitions from one pace to another and fluent delivery of figures and school movements.

- At Stage 2 you will be expected to make active, fluent transitions from trot to canter (and from canter back to trot). The horse will naturally establish the correct sequence of legs in canter for the direction in which he is going, unless he is unbalanced or disturbed by the rider. It is therefore important that you are aware of the correct balance of the horse to enable him to answer your aids with a correct strike-off. (Element 4.2.1)

- It is often easier for the horse to give you a correct strike off in a corner, because here the natural direction of the curve should encourage the horse to take the correct leading leg. On an unfamiliar horse it is therefore advisable to ask for canter in a corner to help ensure that the strike-off is correct.

■ Prepare for the transition to canter well before the corner; think ahead, and take a few strides of sitting trot before the corner. The aids would be:

- apply your inside leg on the girth to maintain and create energy;

- place your outside leg behind the girth to ask the horse to strike off into canter;

- use your inside hand to create a little flexion in the direction in which you are going;

- use your outside hand to regulate the flexion and also control the pace so that the speed of the trot does not increase as you ask for canter.

■ You are likely to be asked to ride such figures as 20m, 15m and perhaps 10m circles, serpentines, loops, turns across the school or down the centre line, and inclines on the long or short diagonal to change the rein. (Element 4.3.1)

How to become competent

■ At the risk of sounding repetitive, the main criterion for competence is **practice**. There is no substitute for practice – 'practice makes perfect'.

■ Ride as many different horses as you can, under instruction and independently, in the school and outside (fields, bridlepaths or any type of off-road hacking).

■ Learn to 'feel' the canter. In the early stages you may need to 'look' for the leading leg in canter, which is preferable to failing to recognise if you are on the incorrect lead and allowing the horse, and even encouraging him, to keep cantering in an unbalanced way.

■ The more you prepare the horse and the more clearly you apply the correct aids, the more likely the horse is to respond obediently and give you the correct lead.

■ Until you can 'feel' the correct leg, learn to glance down to check the leading leg without this affecting your whole position. Gradually learn to recognise the unbalanced feeling you get from the horse when he is on the incorrect lead.

- If the horse does strike off on the 'wrong leg' this is not a major problem as long as you deal with it in a constructive way. Always bring the horse back to trot as soon as you recognise that the lead is incorrect. Rebalance the trot, and re-establish the rhythm and control of the trot. Then prepare again and in an appropriate corner ask for the canter again. If you do this, you will be given far more credit for taking control of the incorrect lead, than if you panic and try to chase the horse back into canter at any price. The chances are he will offer the incorrect lead again because you have not rebalanced and prepared him more clearly.

- Riding good school figures and movements comes with practice. First you must understand the figure you are trying to ride and exactly where it should be positioned in the school. Sometimes it can help you to draw the various school movements on a piece of graph paper so that you can visualise the 'floor pattern'. Draw a 20m by 40m rectangle (to represent a standard arena) and put in the markers (arena letters) in the appropriate positions. Then outline the various

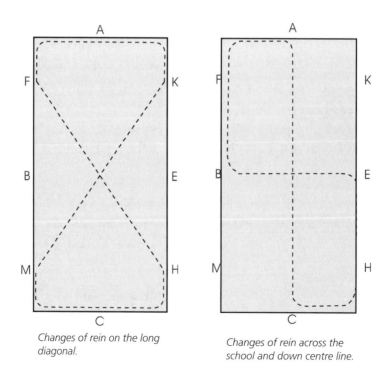

Changes of rein on the long
diagonal.

Changes of rein across the
school and down centre line.

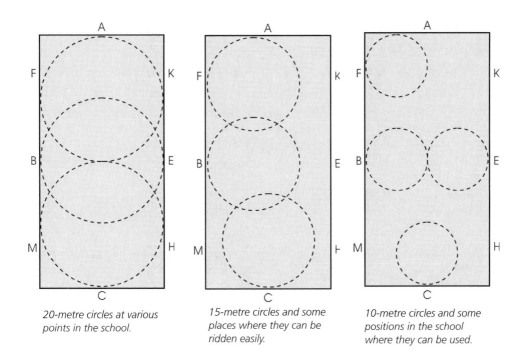

20-metre circles at various points in the school.

15-metre circles and some places where they can be ridden easily.

10-metre circles and some positions in the school where they can be used.

figures in such a way that you can see exactly where they fit in the arena. Commit this to memory and it should help you when you next come to ride the figures on a horse.

- Make sure that you know the aids for basic transitions, figures and movements. If you are familiar with the aids then you should not be struggling to remember which leg goes where. If you are not sure, then the overall communication with the horse will be affected and this will be mirrored in your performance.

- Preparation is a key word. While you can rarely prepare too much, your preparation must remain subtle (especially the thought process) so that the horse does not start to anticipate and react before you ask him. It is very easy, however, not to make enough preparation, which will result in a loss of harmony or effect, or both.

- Some horses will give you a better 'feel' than others. As already mentioned, feel comes with practice and needs nurturing and developing. Each horse you ride will give you a slightly different feeling and therefore each new horse you ride should teach you something a little different.

The candidate should be able to:

Ride in harmony a quiet, experienced horse.

ELEMENT

S   **5.1.1** Demonstrate calm, confident riding in establishing horse's trust.

S   **5.2.1** Show fluent, unconstrained work of the horse.

What the examiner is looking for

- You must try to ride with confidence and demonstrate your competence at this level. This will enable the horse to relax and work with you and then harmony will be the result. (Element 5.1.1)

- Try to forget that you are riding in an exam in front of people assessing your competence. Imagine you are riding a new horse at home and you are keen to find out about him and are enjoying the challenge of learning something new about him. Work to a clear system with thought and preparation for all you do. The horse will then respond to your consistency and the result should be a partnership. (Element 5.2.1)

- Fluent, unconstrained work will be reflected in forward, rhythmical paces in walk, trot and canter. The work should look smooth, accurate and well prepared, with the horse moving easily from one movement to another through clearly recognisable figures and changes of rein.

- You must look as if your whole concentration is on achieving a partnership with the horse; you want to be seen as effective and relaxed in your quest for good, consistent work.

How to become competent

- Become familiar with riding lots of different horses under instruction and independently. Learn to 'feel' the horse and 'read' the horse so that you understand why he might be responding (or not) to you.

- Develop confidence in your ability to be more effective with lazy horses and to be tactful and quiet on 'sharper' horses. Reward the horse with a pat on the neck (or a quiet word) when he responds to you in a positive way, particularly if you have had to use the whip to create a reaction.

- Be aware of what is forward, rhythmical and harmonious and what is tense, anxious and hurried or lazy and 'behind the leg'.

The candidate should be able to:

Ride and jump, adopting safe procedures throughout.

ELEMENT

C **6.1.1** Demonstrate ability to ride safely in company.

S **6.1.2** Demonstrate awareness of rules for riding in enclosed areas with others.

C **6.2.1** Demonstrate an appropriately balanced position when riding over undulating ground.

C **6.3.1** Show an ability to ride forward and influence gaits appropriately when riding in the open.

S **6.3.2** Demonstrate an awareness of undulating ground and weather conditions on a horse's balance.

What the examiner is looking for

- Safe riding develops with knowledge and control. (Element 6.1.1) You must be aware of, and abide by, the rules for riding in enclosed areas with other riders. (Element 6.1.2)

- As a novice rider your instructor will take most, if not all, of the responsibility for your safety while on the horse. This responsibility is something that increasingly becomes yours as your ability as a rider develops.

Illustration of some of the rules for riding in company in an enclosed area.

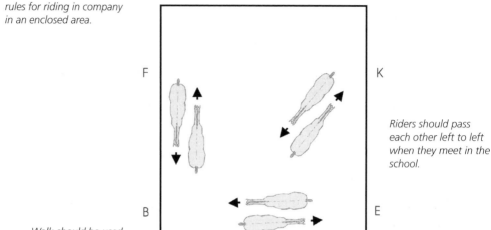

Riders should pass each other left to left when they meet in the school.

Walk should be used on the inner track, giving priority to those trotting or cantering on the track.

trot and canter

walk

- Awareness is essential for you to begin to recognise a potentially unsafe situation and to avoid putting yourself in such a position. (For example, riding too close to the horse in front puts you and/or your horse at risk of being kicked.)

- Control of your horse comes through preparation (including that all-important process: thinking ahead), with clear execution of aids to enable you to clearly influence the horse with good timing.

- Rules for enclosed riding areas include:

- a procedure for entering and leaving the arena, especially when other riders are using the school;

- passing other riders left hand to left hand;

- giving way to others in a faster pace or more difficult movement;

- being aware of riders who may be in difficulty and giving them space to regain control.

■ You must show balance and harmony with the horse in an open space, a large grass field or similar unmarked area. (Element 6.2.1)

■ The position adopted would be appropriate to the pace in which you choose to ride. (Element 6.2.1)

■ You may feel the need to ride with your stirrups one or two holes shorter than you would in the school, when riding on the flat.

■ Whether riding on a dressage saddle or a general-purpose saddle you **may** choose to adopt a slightly lighter seat or jumping position; however, an upright position is also perfectly acceptable. (Element 6.2.1)

■ The emphasis **must** be on the rider's balance and feel of moving with the horse.

■ The rider must show judgement and choose the appropriate pace for riding over undulating ground, taking into account the ground conditions. (Elements 6.3.1 and 6.3.2)

Maintaining a balanced position with the horse going up and down hill.

How to become competent

- The chances are that the establishment where you ride and/or train has a specific set of rules by which it expects its riders (you) to abide. Make sure that you have studied these and that you apply them every time you ride in the school in company.

- Be prepared to adhere specifically to the guidelines which are there to ensure your safety and that of the horse you are riding and other riders around you.

- If in doubt as to your control when riding in company, always reduce your pace first. This gives you a better chance to maintain or regain control of your horse.

- Always ride purposefully and forward. If you ride cautiously in company, sometimes your horse will become nervous and be inclined to spook away from other horses approaching him, only because you are not riding him confidently and making him feel secure.

- When riding in company in an enclosed area, learn to look ahead and gauge when to circle away into space if you are becoming too close to another rider.

- The more you practise riding independently in a school in open order with other riders, the more capable and safe you will be.

- The more you can hack out on different horses, experience riding along bridleways, common land, moorland, beach or forest land the better. This will develop your self-sufficiency and the initiative to 'manage' any circumstances which arise.

- Riding out and about will teach you to 'feel' the horse's balance under you and to learn to adapt your position to enable him to carry you with maximum comfort and minimum effort and inconvenience.

- Riding other than in a 'controlled' marked-out arena under the direction of your instructor, will enable you to 'experiment' with your position and help you to learn to feel when the horse manages you most easily.

- In the school continue to practise plenty of work without stirrups to further deepen your position.

- Practise walk trot and canter without stirrups, and also without stirrups in jumping position.

- Practise changing your position from upright to jumping position and back again in all three gaits.

- Ride outside at different times of the year and learn to feel how a horse balances himself when the ground is deep, slippery or hard.

- Learn to recognise the difference in how the horse moves from one gait to another when he is finding it more difficult to maintain balance on awkward ground.

- Watch other riders riding in difficult conditions and see how they adjust their pace or their position to help the horse.

The candidate should be able to:

Jump a quiet, experienced horse with an appropriate rein length and contact, correct length stirrups and ability to use the legs.

ELEMENT

S **7.1.1** Demonstrate an appropriate length of stirrup for riding over undulating ground and around a course of fences.

C **7.2.1** Show effective use of leg aids when riding over undulating ground and around a course of fences.

C **7.3.1** Show correct application of rein aids when riding over undulating ground and around a course of fences.

S **7.3.2** Show correct use of the reins during all phases of the jump (approach, take-off, flight, landing and departure).

What the examiner is looking for

- As discussed on page 101 regarding Elements 6.3.1 and 6.3.2, you must demonstrate control of the horse and balance in your position. It is likely that taking your stirrups up one or two holes will enable you to demonstrate this balance and control when riding outside on undulating ground (Element 7.1.1) and in due course for jumping a course of fences.

- Your balanced position in harmony with the horse is tested throughout all these Elements (Elements 7.1.1, 7.2.1 and 7.3.1).

- You must show co-ordination in your leg and rein aids but also show effectiveness with your legs to sustain a fluent, forward pace for your riding outside and your course when jumping.

- Rein aids must demonstrate balance and **feel**.

- You must show harmony and control in all phases of the jump as specified in Element 7.3.2.

How to become competent

- There is no substitute for **practice**. Ride as many different horses as possible, particularly out and about in fields, and go out hacking or off-road riding. Develop balance and co-ordination in all paces. Include some faster canter work if you can, so that you learn to balance with a shorter stirrup and broader base of position, which gives you the security to work at faster paces and to jump.

- You must jump as often as you can so that it is familiar to you and not something you do just to prepare for your exam.

- If you can do some pleasure rides, cross-country schooling, or any form of jumping competition, this will develop your competence, familiarity with riding out of the comfort zone of the indoor/

Jumping position with slight variations on upper body angle, which may be used on different horses or in show jumping or cross-country riding.

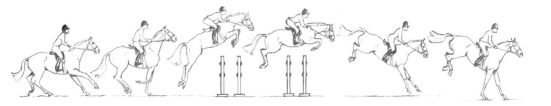

Rider position demonstrated through the phases of the horses' jump from approach, take off, in flight in the air, to landing and departure.

outdoor school, and therefore your confidence.

- Make sure that your instructor supervises your work and checks your position from time to time. This will ensure that you are working in the best balance possible and that you have made best use of the appropriate stirrup length, which as a rough guide should be one to two holes shorter than your normal 'flat-work' riding length.

The candidate should be able to:

Jump a quiet, experienced horse with security and balance, showing fold and follow over a fence.

ELEMENT

| C | **8.1.1** Demonstrate correct forward jumping position when riding over undulating ground and around a course of fences. |

| C | **8.1.2** Demonstrate a secure position when jumping. |

| C | **9.1.1** Show effective control of pace. |

| C | **9.2.1** Identify when and when not to use artificial aids (whip). |

What the examiner is looking for

- The key here is 'security and balance'. Very simply if you are secure through a supple, well-established position on the flat, which then enables you to ride in a good balance over undulating ground and follow the horse fluently when jumping, then you will be demonstrating competence at Stage 2 level. (Elements 8.1.1 and 8.1.2)

- It is important that you can show an understanding of the effective control of pace. The horse should be active and obediently forward, without being either lazy or too 'sharp' and then running against the hand and compromising the rider's control and authority. (Element 9.1.1)

- It is important that you demonstrate an attempt to achieve harmony with the horse. If he is lazy then you must show a clear pathway to be able to influence him with authority so that he responds. This may involve the well-timed use of the whip. (Element 9.2.1) It is just as important that after using the whip, and, it is hoped, achieving a response, you praise the horse (with a pat on the neck or words of encouragement). He then understands the aid you have given and he has been reassured by the praise, being aware that the use of the whip is a reminder to obey the leg aid, not a punishment.

Rider in balance over a fence.

How to become competent

- By working to improve your basic riding position with frequent work without stirrups, ongoing training from your instructor and as much riding as possible on a variety of horses, your depth and security will gradually get better and better. In conjunction with this, taking your stirrups up one or two holes and practising the jumping position in all three gaits will develop your feel and balance in the light seat position.

- An excellent exercise to improve this overall balance and competence is to work in trot and canter in a 'standing up' position. This will ensure that you both 'feel' your balance and develop it, because you can only do this exercise well if you have achieved that balance and flexibility over your lower leg.

- Ride without stirrups, both in your ordinary flatwork and also in pole work (during which you can practise jumping position without stirrups). Gradually work without stirrups over small jumps, and eventually aim to feel more secure and independent without your stirrups than you do with them.

- Riding a horse without a saddle (bareback) also improves your feel and balance. You cannot 'grip' to stay on, as this will inevitably cause you to slip and slide around. Riding bareback encourages you to relax and move with the movement of the horse, because it is easy to feel the horse's movement directly underneath you. It is wise, though, to ride bareback in an enclosed, controlled situation on a horse you know well.

Riding bareback, on a horse you know well, will improve your balance, feel and security.

The candidate should be able to:

Jump in harmony a quiet, experienced horse, whilst riding correct lines of approach towards and departures from fences.

ELEMENT

S **10.1.1** Show effective calm confident riding while jumping.

C **10.2.1** Show a fluently ridden course.

S **10.3.1** Demonstrate awareness of the importance of correct canter leads.

What the examiner is looking for

- Your jumping will be assessed on two horses. On the first horse you will work over one or two small jumps, which will be built up gradually. You may start with a cross-pole (with or without a placing pole) and you will probably be asked to approach in trot.

- Aim to have enough energy in the trot approach so that the horse jumps the fence actively and lands in canter. He should have enough impulsion to maintain the canter fluently as he moves away from the jump.

- If two jumps are then built up, it is likely that there will be one or two non-jumping strides between the first and second jump. The two jumps are regarded as a small 'grid' exercise.

- You should show an ability to create an active approach but not allow the horse to hurry or take control. Keep the horse straight through the centre of the jumps and maintain a good feel and balance in the approach, over the fence and in the departure. (Element 10.1.1)

- This work will then follow into the riding of a small course of about 2ft 6ins (76cm). Your ability to keep a fluent pace around the jumps will be assessed. You must show that you can ride straight lines of approach and departure, keeping the horse energetic around corners, in readiness for presentation to the next jump. (Element 10.2.1)

- The fluency and smoothness of the course will be affected if the horse is unbalanced, particularly around corners. This may be evident by a wrong leading leg in canter. (Element 10.3.1) An incorrect lead is not a point of failure in itself. If the horse is on the wrong leg, particularly if this happens repeatedly, and you show no apparent awareness of the bad effect it is having on him, then this would be considered a weakness at this level.

How to become competent

- You must try to ride and jump several different horses, inside and out. Learn to 'feel' how the horse is moving underneath you. While you may need to 'look' for the leading leg to start with, in time, and with practice, you should develop an increasing awareness of whether the lead is correct or not.

- Try to 'feel' the influence of such things as different 'going' underfoot, gradients, and foothold. Particularly in the 'field,' recognise how the horse changes his way of going to be able to balance himself (and you on top) up and down hills, in heavy going such as deep mud or plough, on hard ground or a slippery surface. Notice if in canter the horse changes leg or becomes disunited, or even loses the canter, because of the ground conditions.

- Once you begin to notice the changes then you can feel how **your** balance affects the horse, and begin to ride with an increasing awareness of maintaining the horse's balance and impulsion.

- Practise your jumping whenever possible. Try to make sure that you ride horses that are genuine and honest to a fence. Horses that maintain a steady and consistent rhythm to the fence are ideal because you should not be disturbed and seeking to regain your balance within the last few strides in front of the fence.

Questions and Answers

It is recommended that you obtain a copy of *The BHS Examinations Handbook*. This useful publication gives you important information relevant to all levels of BHS examinations. It gives a section on each exam, which lists requirements for that level of exam and a suggested programme for the day.

It has a comprehensive list at each level of suggested questions which might be used by examiners during the exam day. Often examiners use the exact question or make some adaptation of situation or wording but the knowledge required is the same if the question is slightly changed.

Below are some of the suggested questions/tasks from the handbook on the Stage 2 syllabus. Each question is listed with a concise answer offering acceptable knowledge. In every case you should try to enhance your answer to give a more comprehensive indication of your depth of knowledge. A more expansive answer requires that you study each subject a little more deeply, which will enable you to speak with greater confidence in giving your answers.

Shoeing

Q. What procedure does the farrier follow when shoeing a horse?
A. Tie up the horse.
Remove the shoes using buffer, hammer and pincers.
Trim the foot for excess horn growth.
Prepare the shoe and the foot for the new shoe.
Nail on the shoe starting at the toe and working on alternate sides to the heels.
Hammer down the clenches and rasp the finished foot lightly, to produce a smooth end-result.

Q. What problems arise from leaving shoes on too long?
A. The foot will overgrow the shoe and there might be injury or lameness.
The shoe may embed into the foot and cause corns or other pressure points, and discomfort.
The shoe may loosen and move on the foot or be pulled off.
The horse's foot balance is affected by shoes that are not maintained and this could cause lameness.

Clipping and Trimming

Q. Why do we need to clip horses?

A. Horses are clipped usually in the winter when they develop a thick protective winter coat. When they are worked they sweat profusely under their thick coat and then may get cold when drying off. Clipping enables the horse to work comfortably with less sweating.

Q. When and how often might they need clipping?

A. Horses usually need clipping any time from mid September onwards, depending on how quickly their winter coat comes through. They usually need clipping every three weeks until the end of the year and then less frequently in the early part of the New Year when the winter coat has stopped growing.

Q. What types of clip are there and when might they be used?

A. The following clips might be used: trace clip, chaser clip, blanket clip, hunter clip, full clip, 'neck and tum'. Different clips are used according to what type of work the horse might be doing. The harder the work, the more the horse is clipped.

Q. What types of clipping machines are available?

A. There are large commercial type machines for clipping many horses. There are smaller electric clippers with blades of different grades coarseness/fineness.There are small battery operated clippers which are quieter for nervous horses or for use around the head.

Q. What checks would you make before use?

A. Check the machine is well maintained, oiled and has been serviced. Make sure that you have a sharp pair of blades.
Make sure the flex is complete and undamaged.
Make sure you are using a circuit breaker for the electrical source.
Make sure that you have a safe stable in which to tie the horse.
Make sure you have assistance available in case you need help.

Q. What care do they need before, during and after use?

A. Machines should be annually checked and serviced. Blades should be resharpened. During clipping regularly turn off the machine so that it does not get too hot and is allowed to cool down. Remove the blades and wipe them and oil them before replacing them. After use the blades should be cleaned, oiled and stored separately while the machine is cleaned of all hair and then oiled and put away.

Q. Why should a circuit breaker be used and where should it be positioned?

A. A circuit breaker protects the user of an electrical appliance from receiving a shock in the event of a problem in the power source. It should be fitted in the plug socket and then the clippers plug is inserted into it.

Anatomy and Physiology

Q. Discuss the health, condition and fitness of a horse.

A. Be able to talk about a horse in front of you, making observations about its state of health/well-being (shiny flexible coat/clear bright eyes/alert/at ease/carrying an appropriate amount of weight for the work it is doing).

Be able to discuss the fitness of the horse i.e. its ability to carry out work. (muscle tone/weight/'clean' legs/'cool' legs.)

Q. How does a horse gather food into his mouth?

A. He 'picks' with his lips, tears with his front (incisor) teeth and then pushes the food into the mouth and towards his back (molar) teeth with his tongue.

Q. What are the functions of the following: the lips, the incisor teeth, the tongue, the molar teeth?

A. The lips – pick the food (grass).
The incisor teeth - tear or cut the food.
The tongue – pushes food to the back of the mouth.
The molar teeth – grind or pulverise the food.

Q. What is the alimentary canal?

A. The digestive tract of the horse from his mouth to his anus.

Q. Where is the gullet?

A. In the horse's neck joining his mouth to his stomach.

Q. What is its other name?

A. The oesophagus.

Q. Can you point it out on the horse?

A. Underside of the neck.

Q. When the horse is eating can you feel and observe when the food passes down the gullet?

A. Yes.

Q. What size is the horse's stomach?

A. Approximately the size of a rugby football with a capacity of 9–18 litres (2–4 gals).

Q. What influence does the size of the stomach have on the way the horse is fed and worked?

A. Due to a relatively small stomach in comparison to the horse's size, he must be fed small amounts of food at a time, so that the volume capacity of the stomach is not overloaded. Frequent small amounts of food will mimic the way the horse would browse naturally in the wild and therefore be most compatible with keeping him healthy.

Q. How long is it before food entering the horse leaves the stomach?

A. This process begins after approximately one hour, but it is ongoing and for the stomach to completely empty its contents will take up to 24 hours. However the stomach should have an ongoing supply of food regularly coming into it.

Q. What are the parts of the alimentary canal after the stomach?

A. The stomach is followed by the small intestine which is made up of three parts: the duodenum, the jejunum and the ileum. The small intestine opens into the large intestine which is made up of the caecum, the large colon, the small colon and then the rectum and the anus.

Q. Why is it important that any change of diet should be introduced slowly?

A. The digestive process in the large intestine is assisted by the presence of 'gut flora' – microbes which help to break down the food into its component parts. If the diet is suddenly changed some of these 'good' microbes may not be able to process the 'new' food and some may not be present that are necessary for the digestion of the 'new' food. Gradual change of diet allows the appropriate microbes to be maintained or evolved to deal with whatever food enters the digestive tract.

Q. Horses cannot be sick (vomit). Is this a disadvantage?

A. Yes, because they are unable to get rid of anything which might be alien or damaging to them other than passing it right through the system which inevitably takes time and may render them fairly ill in the meantime.

Q. Designate the following parts of the horse's skeleton on the horse in front of you:

1. The mandible or jawbone, the occipital bone, the atlas, the axis.

2. The cervical vertebrae and their number. (7 cervical vertebrae, the atlas, the axis and five more.)

3. The thoracic vertebrae and their number. (18 thoracic vertebrae.)

4. The lumbar vertebrae and their number. (6 lumbar vertebrae.)

5. The sacral vertebrae and their number. (5 sacral vertebrae.)

6. The coccygeal vertebrae and their number. (15 to 21 coccygeal vertebrae.)

7. What are the spinal processes? These are bony vertical and transverse extensions of the vertebrae which aid muscle attachment.

8. Where is the sternum? In the chest, between the ribs. **What else may it be called?** Also called the 'breast bone'.

9. Where are the ribs? How many are there? Why are some described as true ribs and some as false ribs? The ribs are in the chest cavity, there are 18 pairs and those that are attached to the spine **and** the sternum are called 'true' ribs (8 pairs); those attached to the spine and only cartilage at the other end are known as 'false or floating' ribs (10 pairs).

10. Name and designate the bones of the forehand. Head, neck, shoulders and forelegs, as far as the withers; skull, cervical vertebrae, shoulder, humerus, radius, carpus, cannon bone, splint bones (2), sesamoids (2), long and short pastern, navicular and pedal bones.

11. **Name and designate the bones which form the hind leg of the horse**.
    Pelvis, femur, fibula, tibia, patella, stifle joint, hock joint, os calcis, then
    from the cannon bone down the limb is the same as the foreleg.

12. **Where is the equivalent on the horse of the human joints of the
    knee, wrist, ankle and elbow?** Knee = horse's patella/stifle; wrist = horse's
    knee; ankle = horse's hock; elbow = horse's elbow.

**Q. Describe the structure of the horse's foot and designate the external
parts?**

A. The horse's foot is like an enclosed box with all the internal structures held
within the horny outer hoof.

Be able to point to: the wall, coronary band, bulbs of the heels, sole, frog,
bars, white line, pastern, and fetlock joint.

Q. What is the function of the frog?

A. It is the 'shock-absorber' for the foot, adding 'grip' when it contacts the
ground, and it assists in pushing the blood back up the leg to maintain
circulation.

Q. Why is the white line so important?

A. It shows externally the join between the insensitive parts and the sensitive
parts of the foot.

Q. What daily care is needed to keep the feet healthy?

A. The feet must be picked out at least twice each day and the foot checked
carefully to notice its condition. The ongoing state of the shoes, if the horse
is shod, should be noticed. Oiling the feet two or three times a week helps to
maintain supple, healthy horn and a good appearance.

Q. What problems arise from neglect of the feet?

A. The feet may smell and then gradually become infected due to not being
cleaned out well. Injury, due to the presence of stones or sharp objects not
removed by cleaning, may make the horse lame. Lack of observation of the
condition of the shoes can lead to injury or lameness.

Horse Health

Q. How do the following headings tell us about the horse's health or ill-health?

1. Breathing. Breathing should be regular and quiet with a rest rate of approximately 8 to 12 in a healthy horse. Raised respiration without reason such as exercise or excitement, or accompanied by other signs such as sweating or pain, would indicate a possible problem with the horse's health.

2. Eating. A healthy horse eats consistently, confidently and thrives on its food. Changes in eating habits for no visible reason accompanied by other worrying signs such as discomfort, change in droppings or behaviour may indicate an onset of ill-health.

3. Excreting. A healthy horse passes well-formed, greenish brown droppings on a regular basis. A change in colour, consistency or smell of droppings, or more infrequent or profuse passing, may indicate the onset of ill health.

4. Lying down. A content, confident horse may lie down to rest. Knowing your horse's normal habits is important in assessing when there is abnormal behaviour. Resting a hind leg is quite normal, and it is usual for the horse to rest both hind legs alternately. Some horses rest a hind leg with the opposite diagonal foreleg resting too – this again is quite normal if it is something that the horse does regularly. Abnormal stance or the development of a 'new' resting habit might cause you to consider whether there was a problem. Horses can relax and sleep standing up.

5. Moving, turning and backing. Horses should move easily around both the field and their stable; they should turn both ways and back up as required. Any change in their ability to move confidently and with ease should be investigated.

Horse Behaviour – At Grass

Q. When feeding horses in the field, how may they behave?

A. They may move around fractiously trying to be the first to get the food; they may threaten each other with ears back and sometimes turning their hindquarters to threaten a kick in their efforts to establish superiority.

Q. What is meant by 'pecking order'?

A. The horses' desire to establish the 'head of the herd' and lower order of hierarchy by threatening each other until the lower order submit to the authority of the 'leader of the pack'. Horses lower in the pecking order will 'submit' to those above them.

Q. How do you make sure they can sort out safely their natural 'pecking order'?

A. Make sure when feeding the horses that there are more piles of food available than the number of horses, and that the food is spaced well enough apart, so that the 'boss' cannot bully the other horses away from the food. When introducing a newcomer into the group make sure that the new horse meets one or two from the group first before being put in with them all. Keep large groups of horses unshod behind so that they do not injure each other. Keep mares and geldings separately so that the 'boys' don't fight over the 'girls'.

Q. How would you know your horse was worried by flies and needed to be brought into the stable?

A. Horses running around fractiously, with visible signs of biting flies in the area of the horses. Horses in warm weather not settling and either grazing or resting in the shade. Horses showing anxiety and intermittently running about, sometimes in a quite a frenzy and disturbed state.

Horse Behaviour – In the Stable

Q. A new horse comes into the yard and is very unsettled. What precautions would you take to ensure his safety during the time he takes to settle down?

A. Keep him in a large well-bedded-down stable with nothing on which he might injure himself. Give him a plentiful supply of hay to occupy him and keep him next to another horse who is very calm and settled to try to influence the new horse. Make sure that the person looking after the horse is competent and reassuring to try to help the horse to settle. Perhaps leave stable bandages on him for protection.

Q. In what way do we go against the natural habitat of the horse when we stable him?

A. Keep him individually rather than in a herd or group.

Feed him intermittently rather than let him graze at will.

Confine him rather than allow him to wander at will.

Prevent him from exercising himself.

Restrict the interest factor in his life.

Restrict physical contact with other horses.

Q. How would you describe a nervous horse?

A. Unsettled, standing at the door looking anxious, not eating or resting calmly, may pace around the box and show disturbance whenever anything else happens in the yard.

Q. How is a nervous horse likely to react when you enter his stable?

A. He may move to the back of the box, turning his bottom towards you and not wishing to greet you. He may not want to be caught.

Q. How would you approach a nervous horse?

A. Calmly, with reassuring words and a quiet well-timed pat; perhaps take a small tit-bit (carrot or apple) to tempt him and show that you are friendly.

Q. What sort of things that are done to a stabled horse are likely to upset him?

A. Anything unusual or not done regularly. Possibly, clipping, treating a wound or injury, tail or mane pulling. Anything new or using equipment that is unfamiliar to him.

Q. What sort of behaviour would make you think that a horse is going to be difficult to handle in his box?

A. He goes to the back of the box when you approach.

He is miserable with ears back and bad tempered manner when you meet him over the door.

Difficult to catch in the box.

Bad manners or bad temper once you have the head collar on (biting, barging, swinging his quarters towards you).

Q. What kind of behaviour in the stable would indicate that the horse when turned out might be difficult to catch?

A. Difficult to catch in the stable, anxious and timid to handle.

Q. What sort of happenings around the yard are likely to upset a stabled horse?

A. Loud noises or unexpected noises or sudden happenings. Another horse being removed from next door to an anxious horse.

Q. How can you calm a nervous horse?

A. Stable him next to a calm horse.

Ensure a consistent routine of management.

Spend time with him reassuring him and grooming him.

Put him in a quiet part of the yard but with other horses around him.

Have a competent, calm reassuring person to look after him.

The Horse When Ridden

Q. When being ridden, how will a horse show he is excited?

A. He may bounce or prance about, not stay relaxed and forward in a rhythm; he may try to run off.

Q. When commencing exercise, some horses will kick out. What does this behaviour demonstrate?

A. Anxiety to 'get moving'. Perhaps threatening other horses around him and invading his 'space'. Tension due to lack of exercise.

Q. How might your horse behave if his tack does not fit him?
   (a) The saddle?
   (b) The bridle?

A. (a) Reaction to a poorly fitting saddle may be shown in tension through the back when being ridden; at worst the horse may buck or try to run away; he may dip his back away when the rider mounts or just not want to go forward at all.

(b) The horse may show reluctance to go forward if the bridle is ill-fitting; if the problem is in his mouth, he may show resistance and discomfort in the mouth, and at worst he may rear. He may put his head up and avoid having the bridle put on at all.

Q. How would you behave towards your horse to get the best out of him at all times?

A. With kindness, calmness and consistency in all your actions. The horse must always understand what is being expected or asked of him. He must be rewarded often when he is genuine and accepting and corrected with understanding, firmness and clarity when he is disobedient or naughty.

Taking the Exam

You will probably already be familiar with the protocol of a BHS examination if you have taken Stage 1. If you are coming to Stage 2 through exemption by completing Progressive Riding Tests 1 to 6 or through any other dispensation, then this may be the first BHS exam you have been involved in.

Exam psychology

- Believe in yourself and your ability to pass the exam.

- Continually remind yourself of all the preparation and practice you have put in prior to this day.

- Continually tell yourself that you will not be asked to do anything or asked a question on anything that is not totally familiar to you.

- Remember that you will know enough; you just have to show the examiners that knowledge. They cannot assume your competence or guess how much you know, you have to keep showing them and telling them.

Exam procedure

- The exam will take all day. Usually the riding on the flat and jumping takes place in the morning, followed by the lungeing. The stable management will be split into three sections:

    practical,
    practical oral, and
    theory

Often one section of practical stable management, one theory section and one section of riding on the flat will rotate.

- There can be up to six candidates in each stable management group; sometimes a group may be made up of candidates sitting only the care section of the exam, while others may be taking only the riding section. There can be

STAGE 2 – TIMETABLE/PROGRAMME

PROGRAMME A

Up to 15 Riding/18 Care

	Ride	Practical/Oral	Practical
9.00–10.25	Group A	Group B	Group C
10.25–11.50	Group B	Group C	Group A
11.50–1.15	Group C	Group A	Group B
1.15	LUNCH		
2.15	**Lungeing (3/4 hr)** (3 horses if 20 x 60 arena available)		**Theory**
	1–9		10–18
3.00	10–18		1–9
3.45	Exam ends (results as soon as possible)		

PROGRAMME B

Up to 15 Riding/18 Care

	Ride	Practical	**Lunge & Theory** (1/2 hr lunge – 3 horses if 20 x 60 arena available)
9.00–10.25	Group A	Group B	Group C
10.25–11.50	Group B	Group C	Group A
11.50–1.15	Group C	Group A	Group B
1.15	LUNCH		
pm	3 groups x 3 horses x 3 examiners		
2.15–3.15	**Practical/Oral** (Candidates change examiners after 20 mins)		
	Exam ends (results as soon as possible)		

PROGRAMME C

Up to 15 Riding/18 Care

	Ride	Theory	Practical/Oral
9.00	Group A	Group B	Group C
9.55	Group B	Group C	Group A
10.50	Group C	Group A	Group B

	Jumping	**Lungeing (3 horses)**
11.45	1–8	9–16
12.30	9–16	1–8
1.15	LUNCH	
2.15	**Practical – all candidates**	
3.15	Exam ends (results as soon as possible)	

This programme is only suitable where the Centre is able to provide enough horses and equipment for the practical, with all candidates together pm.

When one group is riding ONLY it can also be suitable.

PROGRAMME D

Up to 15 Riding/ 18 Care

	Ride/Jump	Practical	Practical Oral (or Theory)
9.00	Group A (riding only)	Group B	Group C
9.50	Group A (jump)	Group C	Group B
10.35	Sum up and results for Group A		

	Ride		Lunge (2 examiners)
11.00	Group B (flat only)		Group C 3 horses in 20 x 60m **or** 2 horses in 20 x 40m plus 1 horse in another area
11.50	Group C (flat only)		Group B
12.40	LUNCH		

	Jump (2 horses each)		Practical Oral (or Theory)
1.40	Group B		Group C
2.30	Group C		Group B
3.20 approx	Exam ends (results as soon as possible)		

Where the Centre has school and jumping areas adjacent the programme could be:

	Ride Flat and Jump	Lunge and Theory (or Practical Oral)
11.00	Group B	Group C
12.35	LUNCH	
1.35	Group C	Group B
3.10 approx	Exam ends (results as soon as possible)	

up to five candidates in each riding group.

■ Be polite and sociable with other candidates but avoid sharing experiences. If someone tries to tell you about the horses at the centre, politely excuse yourself from the conversation. It is far better that you ride on your own initiative and competence rather than rely on snippets of information, however well meant. A small amount of isolated information about a horse may, in fact, be more of a hindrance, especially if the facts are wrong or you muddle them up with another horse. Similarly, avoid getting into conversations with other candidates who are panicking about 'how difficult the jumps are', or that 'the lunge horses are lazy', or that 'Mrs So and So is examining and she doesn't like people with green hair and black nailpolish'! Such discussions can be damaging to your calmness and focus, and you must not get involved in them. Maintain your concentration on the day ahead and apply yourself to every situation that arises.

■ If you have a bad experience in any section of the exam (e.g. a horse stops at a fence while jumping, or you drop a stable bandage half-way through applying it) stay calm and repair the situation to the best of your ability. One small mistake will never fail you, even if at the time it feels like a major catastrophe. In all cases it is the way you deal with the incident that indicates your common sense and capability (e.g. with a dropped bandage, remove the whole thing, re-roll quickly and start again).

■ In every section, your examiner will introduce himself/herself and explain what he or she is expecting in that particular part of the exam. You will move around in groups of up to six, but in the practical section of the exam you will tend to be asked to carry out individual tasks or share a task with one other candidate. In the latter case make sure that you tell the examiner what parts of the work you have personally been responsible for. If you are asked to comment on something that you have not been responsible for, make sure that the examiner knows this (especially if a piece of equipment is not correctly fitted). If you have to criticise another candidate's work, do it as tactfully as possible.

■ Make sure that you wear gloves when lungeing or if asked to hold a horse, but make equally sure that you remove your gloves when carrying out 'hands-on' practical tasks (e.g. grooming and fitting tack).

■ Be practical and forthcoming throughout the day; relax, smile and stay comfortable (stay warm and dry, visit the loo if you need to, bring lunch and plenty of fluids to drink).

■ At the end of the day make sure that you collect all your belongings, and give your arm numbers to the examiner in your final section. The results will be sent to you and should arrive within a week to ten days.

Further Reading

The following books and booklets can all be obtained from the BHS Bookshop.

The BHS Complete Manual
of Stable Management

The BHS Veterinary Manual

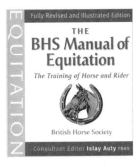

The BHS Manual of
Equitation

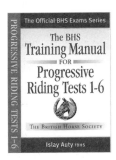

The BHS Training
Manual for
Progressive Riding
Tests 1-6

The BHS Training
Manual for Stage 1

The BHS Training
Manual for Stage 3
and PTT

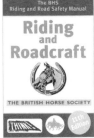

The BHS Riding and
Road Safety Manual –
Riding and Roadcraft

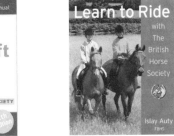

Learn to Ride with
The British Horse
Society

Guide to BHS
Examinations

Examinations
Handbook

BHS Guide to Careers
with Horses

Duty of Care

Useful Addresses

British Horse Society
Stoneleigh Deer Park
Kenilworth
Warwickshire
CV8 2XZ
tel: 08701 202244 or 01926 707700
fax: 01926 707800
website: www.bhs.org.uk
email: enquiry@bhs.org.uk

BHS Examinations Department
(address as above)
tel: 01926 707784
fax: 01926 707800
email: exams@bhs.org.uk

BHS Training Department
(address as above)
tel: 01926 707822
     01926 707821
email: training@bhs.org.uk

**BHS Riding Schools/Approvals
     Department**
(address as above)
tel: 01926 707795
fax: 01926 707796
email: Riding.Schools@bhs.org.uk

BHS Bookshop
(address as above)
tel: 08701 201918
     01926 707762
website: www.britishhorse.com

The BHS Examination System

Outline of progression route through BHS examinations

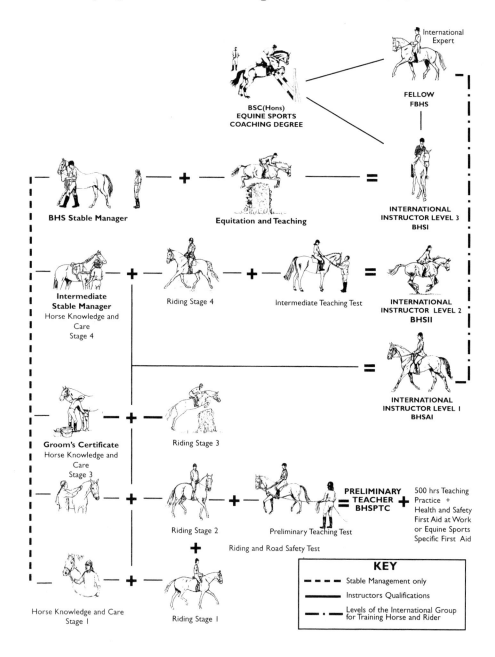

International Expert

BSC(Hons) EQUINE SPORTS COACHING DEGREE

FELLOW FBHS

BHS Stable Manager + **Equitation and Teaching** = **INTERNATIONAL INSTRUCTOR LEVEL 3 BHSI**

Intermediate Stable Manager Horse Knowledge and Care Stage 4 + Riding Stage 4 + Intermediate Teaching Test = **INTERNATIONAL INSTRUCTOR LEVEL 2 BHSII**

= **INTERNATIONAL INSTRUCTOR LEVEL 1 BHSAI**

Groom's Certificate Horse Knowledge and Care Stage 3 + Riding Stage 3

+ Riding Stage 2 + Preliminary Teaching Test **PRELIMINARY TEACHER BHSPTC** + 500 hrs Teaching Practice + Health and Safety First Aid at Work or Equine Sports Specific First Aid

Riding and Road Safety Test

Horse Knowledge and Care Stage 1 + Riding Stage 1

KEY

- - - - Stable Management only

——— Instructors Qualifications

—·—·— Levels of the International Group for Training Horse and Rider